FORD VERSUS FERRARI
The Battle for Le Mans

By the same author
FORMULA ONE
ITALIAN HIGH-PERFORMANCE CARS
(with Keith Davey)

Ford versus Ferrari
The Battle for Le Mans

ANTHONY PRITCHARD

PELHAM BOOKS

First published in Great Britain by
PELHAM BOOKS LTD.
26 Bloomsbury Street
London W.C.1
1968
© 1968 by *Anthony Pritchard*

Reprinted with agreement of the Author and Copyright Holder by
Mercian Manuals Ltd.
353 Kenilworth Road
Balsall Common, Coventry
CV7 7DL
England

Reprint 2001

ISBN 1 903088 09 7

CONTENTS

Introduction   11

1. Le Mans – The Hub of Sports Car Racing   13
2. The Growth of Ferrari Power   23
3. The Modern Ferrari   36
4. The Cobra Factor   46
5. The Evolution of the Ford GT40   57
6. 1964   72
7. 1965   89
8. 1966   111
9. 1967   132

Postscript   154

Appendices:

1. The Performances of Works Ferraris in Sports Car Racing, 1964–67   156
2. The Performances of Works Fords in Sports Car Racing, 1964–67   158
3. The Specification of the Ferrari 275LM and P4   162
4. The Specification of the Ford GT40, Mk II and Mk IV   163

5 Le Mans Winners on Distance, 1923–67   163

Index   171

ILLUSTRATIONS

1	The sole surviving Bentley makes a pit stop on the Sunday morning of the 1927 race	*facing page*	32
2	The 3-litre French Ariès, which so nearly won the 1927 Le Mans event		32
3	The winning 2·3-litre Alfa Romeo of 1931 about to cross the finishing line		33
4	The winning Ferrari in the 1949 Le Mans race		33
5	The Jaguar XK120C, winner of the 1953 race		40
6	The very fierce 4·5-litre Ferrari coupé of 1953		41
7	Mike Hawthorn about to test a 4·9-litre Ferrari of the type which won the 1954 Le Mans race		56
8	Duncan Hamilton about to leave the pits in the second place Jaguar in the 1954 race		56
9	One of Briggs Cunningham's entries in 1953 was this 5454 cc Chrysler-powered car		57
10	The Nash Company's entry in 1953		57
11	The Tipo 246/SP, first of the rear-engined Ferraris which ran at Le Mans in 1961		64
12	The Lola on its last race appearance at Brands Hatch in 1963		64
13	A Shelby American Daytona Coupé at speed in the 1965 Daytona 2,000 kms race		65
14	Race debut for the Ford GT in the 1964 Nurbürgring 1,000 kms race		65

15	The 3-litre Tipo 250/P Ferrari which won the 1964 Nürburgring 1000 kms race	72
16	A Le Mans victory for the 3·3-litre Tipo 275/P Ferrari in 1964	72
17	One of the three Fords which retired at Le Mans in 1964	73
18	One of the Mk II cars powered by 7-litre engines developed by Ford for 1965	88
19	This 4·7-litre open car was entered by Ford France in the 1965 Le Mans race	88
20	John Surtees	89
21	Lorenzo Bandini with team-mate Chris Amon	89
22	Carroll Shelby and Phil Hill discussing 1965 Le Mans prospects	96
23	Bruce McLaren	96
24	The Mk II version of the GT40 which won the Daytona 24-hour race in 1966	97
25	The Ford X-1, an open version of the Mk II, scores a victory in the Sebring 12-hour race in 1966	97
26	The 7-litre Mk II of Bucknum and Hutcherson which finished third in the 1966 Le Mans race	104
27	The 4-litre P3 which Mike Parkes and Lodovico Scarfiotti drove in the 1966 race	104
28	The finish at Le Mans, 1966	105
29	At the Le Mans trials in 1966 Ford introduced the 'J', an experimental design	120
30	For 1967 Ford produced the Mk IV	120
31	Phil Hill seen during the 1966 Le Mans event in the Chaparral	121

32	The 1967 Chaparral, a much improved and redesigned car	121
33	The Lola-Aston, bearer of all British hopes in the 1967 race	128
34	The Ford France-entered Mk II, Le Mans, 1967	128
35	The second place Ferrari in the 1967 Le Mans race	129
36	The Mirage, a modified version of the catalogued GT40 Mk III	129

ACKNOWLEDGMENTS

Although the author accepts full responsibility for the accuracy of the contents of this book, it would not have been possible to compile it without the assistance of many people. It is not possible to list them all here, but especial thanks are due to the Public Relations Department of the Ford Motor Company and to Maranello Concessionaires Ltd. I am also extremely grateful to Keith Davey for his assistance in the preparation of the manuscript.

Thanks are due to the following for permission to reproduce photographs: Nos. 1, 2, 3, 12 *Autocar;* Nos. 4, 5, 9, 10 Louis Klementaski; Nos. 6, 15, 16, 27, 33 *Motor Sport;* No. 7 *Motor Racing;* No. 8 Rodolfo Mailander; No. 11 Geoffrey Goddard; No. 21, *Autosport.*

Introduction

The Grand Prix d'Endurance du Mans is deservedly the World's most famous long-distance motor race. For more than forty years it has attracted a large number of cars from Europe, some of them long forgotten whereas others seem to claim a whole decade to themselves – Bentley the nineteen-twenties, Alfa Romeo the 'thirties, Jaguar the 'fifties and Ferrari the 'sixties. Over the years the struggle between the various contestants has attracted international public interest, and manufacturers involved in racing at the Sarthe circuit have consoled themselves with the belief that their vast expenditure has resulted in increased sales.

The recent struggle for supremacy between Ferrari and Ford was not by any means a new experience for spectators at Le Mans, for they watched a similar struggle in the 'fifties. Nor was it a new experience for Ferrari, for they were one of the participants then also. Enzo Ferrari's own racing experience dates back further than the circuit of La Sarthe itself, and it was he who engineered those great Alfa Romeo victories of more than thirty years ago as 'patron' of the Scuderia Ferrari. He has been racing cars under his own name since 1947, recently with financial aid from the giant Fiat concern, and, since the withdrawal of Aston Martin, Jaguar and Maserati from racing, has swept the board in International racing. Ferrari's approach to racing is a highly emotional one. His numerous rows with race organisers, and with his own technicians and drivers, are matched only by his dogged determination. Time and again Ferraris have been completely outclassed one year, only to return the next year with a better car and a greater determination to win.

Ford, however, are a different proposition. Their sudden interest in racing is, to a large extent, based on commercial reasoning – although the men entrusted with the competitions work are undoubtedly devotees of the sport. Ford philosophy is not so much 'improve the breed' as 'improve the public image', and this has certainly worked if the enormously increased sales of the Mustang are anything to go by. Their racing experience when they started was negligible. The problem they faced was clear-cut; could they *buy* sufficient technical know-how to overcome Ferrari's vast wealth of racing experience.

ONE

Le Mans - The Hub of Sports Car Racing

Initiative for the first ever Le Mans 24-hour race, held in May, 1923, came from Charles Faroux of *La Vie Automobile* and Georges Durand who planned an event of the utmost rigour for production touring cars – the emphasis being on testing the chassis, the general running gear and equipment. Entries were restricted to touring cars conforming in every detail with the manufacturer's current catalogue and properly equipped with wings, running boards, headlamps, tail and side lamps, hood, horn and rear-view mirror. Except for cars of under 1100 cc, 4-seater bodywork was compulsory. All repairs had to be carried out by the driver, but pit staff were permitted to place on the pit counter tools and spare parts as required, and there were no restrictions on fuel except that petrol and oil must be taken on at the pits. For this first race, there was to be no outright winner, but finishers who had covered the prescribed minimum distance qualified for the Rudge Whitworth Triennial Cup the eventual winner being decided in 1925!

With such little inducement to enter and the necessity of paying an entry fee of between 1000 and 2000 francs according to engine capacity, it is surprising that as many as 33 cars should come to the starting line – all French with the exception of a solitary Bentley driven by John Duff and Frank Clement. It is a sobering thought that none of the sixteen makes entered, again with the exception of the Bentley, remains in production today. Although the Bentley was not strictly a works car, Duff was the London Bentley agent, the car had been works prepared and the pit was controlled by W. O. Bentley himself. The early part of the race was held in heavy rain, the road surface soon broke up with the pounding of the cars and became covered with a thick layer of mud. A stone thrown up by a car in front went through one of the Bentley's headlamps and during the night it lost ground to the leading Chenard-Walcker. As daylight broke the Bentley speeded up and moved into the lead, only to run out of fuel on the course because a stone had holed the petrol tank. Eventually fuel was obtained from the pits and the Bentley restarted. At the end of the twenty-four hours it had covered fourth equal distance beaten by two Chenard-Walckers and a Bignan.

Duff's performance at Le Mans was sufficiently encouraging for him to enter the race once again the following year. An additional regulation introduced for 1924 was that drivers of open cars had to stop at the pits after the fifth lap, raise the hood and cover at least two laps with it erect. By holding the race a month later, in June, the organisers secured fine weather and a lot of hard work had been put into improving the road surface. Despite 40 minutes spent in sorting out a jammed gear-lever, despite the windscreen breaking away from its mountings and despite shock-absorber failures, Duff and Clement scored a convincing win from two very powerful 3½-litre Lorraine-Dietrich entries. In 1925 and 1926 Bentley Motors entered official works teams at Le Mans, but in both years all the Bentleys retired and victory went to the Lorraines. It should not be forgotten, however, that in the 1925 event a rare success was scored by one of the beautifully made, but mechanically unreliable Sunbeam 3-litre twin overhead camshaft cars driven by Chassagne and S. C. H. Davis which finished second.

Undeterred by their failures, Bentley returned in force to Le Mans in 1927 with a team which included a new 4½-litre car. Although there were only 22 starters, the Bentleys faced stiff opposition in the form of a very fast 3-litre French Ariès driven by Chassagne and Laly and a new Regulation insisted on all tools and spares being carried on the car; water, oil and petrol could not be taken on until at least 20 laps had been covered. This is no place to repeat in full the old story of how the Bentley 3-litre of Sammy Davis and Dr Benjafield survived the multi-car crash which eliminated the other two team Bentleys and severely damaged their car. The story is told at first hand in *A Racing Motorist* by Davis (Iliffe & Sons, 1949) and well narrated in *A Racing History of the Bentley* by Darrell Berthon (The Bodley Head, 1956 and re-issued by Autobooks in 1962). It suffices to say that despite a bent front axle and chassis, a wrecked mudguard, the loss of one headlamp and, not discovered

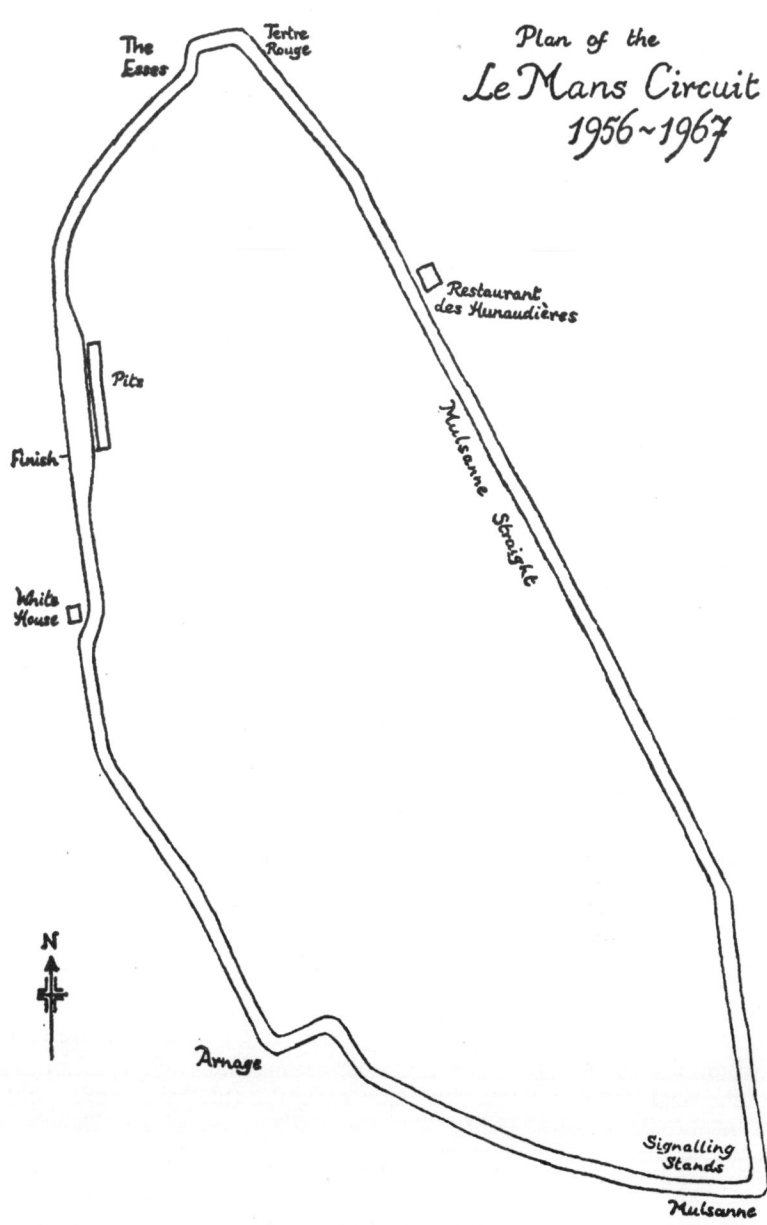

until after the race, a cracked steering arm ball joint, the Bentley continued gradually gaining ground on the leading Ariès that was now six laps ahead. Speeding up the Bentley caused the Ariès to speed up to retain its lead and also caused the hoped for, but not expected, engine failure which gave victory to the British team.

Already the Le Mans race was gaining fame and successful manufacturers advertised their successes and named models in honour of their victories. Bentley naturally made much of their Le Mans Victory and in 1928 the team returned to consolidate their success. For the first time there was to be an Annual Award for the greatest distance covered and for the first time American manufacturers had taken an interest in the race. Among the entries were three Chryslers and a single Stutz Black Hawk. The Stutz was an extremely fast car with a single overhead camshaft straight eight engine of close to 5-litres and had been entered by Charles Weymann of Weymann coachwork fame. Throughout the race the Bentleys were hard pressed by the American cars and at the finish the winning $4\frac{1}{2}$-litre (the car that had been involved in the previous year's crash) of Barnato and Rubin was only eight miles ahead of the Stutz of Brisson and Bloch, which had been slowed by the need to hold top gear in.

The Le Mans organisers had since the inception of the race wanted to eliminate the dangerous Pontlieue hairpin and this was done for the 1929 race by improving and using a private road thereby reducing the circuit length from 10·726 to 10·153 miles. Five Bentleys, four of $4\frac{1}{2}$-litres and a $6\frac{1}{2}$-litre model were entered, Stutz were back in force with three supercharged cars entered by Weymann and other interesting American entries came from Chrysler with two cars and there was a single du Pont. The depression had already hit the French motor industry and none of their factories entered potential winners. One of the Bentleys was eliminated by a broken magneto drive shaft, but otherwise fortune smiled on the Cricklewood entries, while it was a hapless race for the American cars. For much of the race the Bentleys sat comfortably in first four positions, their speed and regularity controlled by the pits, and their triumph was complete, the four cars taking the chequered flag in numerical order. Of the American cars, the du Pont retired with transmission trouble, the Chryslers had to be content with sixth and seventh places, two of the Stutz entries were eliminated by leaking fuel tanks, while the remaining American car, the Stutz of Bouriat and 'Philippe' took a well-earned fifth place.

1930 saw the final appearance of works Bentleys at Le Mans, three 6½-litre Speed Sixes, and of 18 starters, five were Bentleys, for the Hon. Dorothy Paget ran two 4½-litre supercharged cars. Stutz had entered two cars and there was a solitary and vast 7-litre supercharged Mercedes driven by Rudolph Caracciola and Christian Werner. The Mercedes led at the end of the first lap, but was soon caught up in a close duel with Birkin's blown Bentley. After a tyre failed on the Bentley, Caracciola held an early lead until caught and harried by Barnato's works Bentley. Eventually the Mercedes retired with a blown gasket and after tyre and mechanical troubles with the blown cars, victory went to the works Speed Six of Barnato and Kidston. Shortly after this race, the Bentley Company announced their withdrawal from racing and a year later passed into the control of Rolls-Royce. Despite their failures in the 1925 and 1926 races, Le Mans in the 'twenties seemed an era of Bentley domination and of British greatness, but a new order of domination at Le Mans was to come about.

Alfa Romeo had already enjoyed a distinguished competition record with their beautifully constructed twin overhead camshaft P2 Grand Prix cars which had largely dominated Grand Prix racing during 1924 and 1925. These were the work of Vittorio Jano, a former Fiat employee, and his sports cars derived from these had already achieved wins in the 1928 and 1929 Mille Miglia and the 1928 and 1929 Belgian 24-hour races. 1931 saw the appearance of a new Alfa Romeo model, the 8C-2300 with the 2336 cc straight eight engine cast in two blocks of four cylinders and the gears driving the twin overhead camshafts mounted between them. Two of these cars were entered in the 1931 race by the Scuderia Ferrari on behalf of the works and once again there were strong contenders from Stutz and Mercedes-Benz. The winning Alfa, however, was the privately owned but works assisted car of Lord Howe and Tim Birkin, forced to give up their allegiance to the British Racing Green, with a lead of 70 miles over the Mercedes of Boris Ivanowski and Henri Stoffel.

For 1932 further changes to the course were made and the organising club, the Automobile Club d'Ouest, shortened its length to 8·384 miles by building on their own land a road linking the two north/south highways. With weakening opposition, Alfa Romeo continued to dominate the race during the years 1932 to 1934 and the fight for the lead was generally a fight amongst themselves. All these winning Alfas were privately entered, but in receipt of works support, and opposition was limited during these years to British Talbots and the odd American Duesenberg. Although the Talbots were not fast enough to challenge the Alfas for victory, driven by Brian Lewis and Tim Rose – Richards, they took third place in both 1931 and 1932. Only the winning Alfa had finished in the 1934 race and the following year saw a reversal of Alfa fortunes from which they did not recover. Alfas led the field for much of the 1935 race, but a lap-scoring error in the Alfa pits let the 4½-litre Lagonda of Hindmarsh and Fontes into the lead and a well deserved win.

Nation-wide strikes caused the abandonment of the 1936 race, and the following year's race saw a renaissance of French racing power. Strong entries came from Bugatti, Delahaye, Delage and Talbot and victory went to the streamlined so-called 'tank' Bugatti of Jean-Pierre Wimille and Robert Benoist. This superbly aerodynamic and stylish supercharged works car based on the production Type 57SC model set a new lap record of 96·42 mph and covered a record distance of 2043 miles. Bugatti did not enter the 1938 race when victory went to Delahayes which occupied first, second and fourth positions after the retirement of the very much faster supercharged 2·9-litre Alfa Romeo coupé of Sommer and Biondetti. Bugatti returned to Le Mans in 1939 with a solitary entry. This was an improved streamlined version of the 1937 car and based on the production Type 57C touring car. Mechanical modifications were few and it speaks highly for the aerodynamic efficiency of this car that not only did it set a new race distance record of 2084·547 miles at an average of 86·86 mph, but its average fuel consumption was 10·8 mpg. This Bugatti was reckoned to have a top speed of 170 mph and not once during the race was the bonnet opened. Within a matter of weeks the Second World War had broken out.

When Le Mans was liberated by allied troops, the track, used by the Germans as aircraft runways, had been devastated by bombing, the grandstands and buildings were shattered ruins. A formidable task of reconstruction faced the Automobile Club d'Ouest, but new and much improved spectator facilities were provided and the track remade so that by 1949 it was possible to hold the first post-war race. The pre-war years at Le Mans saw, as did sports racing in general, little in the way of technical development. The Bentleys and their contemporaries were solid, robust low-revving cars of tremendous weight. Bentley's prime concession to the need for great power was to enlarge the engine. The beautifully constructed Alfa Romeos were closely related in design to the Grand Prix cars from the Milan factory which were so quickly overhauled in technical development by the German Mercedes-Benz and Auto Union of 1934 onwards. There was not to be seen at Le Mans the engine, chassis and suspension advances which enlivened the Grand Prix scene and advances were primarily limited to the beautifully streamlined forms of the Bugatti of the late 'thirties and to the eccentric forms of such smaller cars as the Chenard-Walckers, Peugeots and Adlers. Notable technical advances, encouraged by relaxation of the Race Regulations so as to permit the running of prototypes that need never enter production were, however, a strong feature of the post-war Le Mans scene.

Despite its enormous spectator appeal in France, Le Mans had yet to attract strong International works teams, it had yet to gather the International following at all levels that makes headline news. It was then as the Tour de France cycle race still is today, a truly National French event, but of interest elsewhere only to enthusiasts. Out of 49 starters in the 1949 mainly the entries of small British and French teams, two were of tremendous significance. These were the 2-litre Ferraris, superbly constructed and complex cars with V-12 engines having a single overhead camshaft per bank of cylinders and the excellent power output of 140 bhp, a tubular chassis, wishbone suspension and an all-enveloping body of superb appearance. Not only did the Ferrari of Lord Selsdon and Luigi Chinetti, now boss of the NART team, win the race from the basically pre-war French Delahayes, Delages and Talbots, but their victory gave a firm and descernible hint of future design trends at Le Mans.

Victory went in 1950 to one of the 'old guard' of French sports cars, a $4\frac{1}{2}$-litre Talbot driven by Louis Rosier and his son Jean-Louis, a car that was virtually a Grand Prix Talbot with wings and lights added, but in essentials little different from the Talbots that had competed at Le Mans in pre-war days. It was in 1951 that the race attracted the first serious International entries since the war and it was the presence of important teams from Britain and the United States that began to give the race International interest. The British contingent was led by a team of works Jaguar XK120Cs, the Coventry concern's first model designed specifically for competition work, with Jaguar's superb 3442 cc 6-cylinder engine and a beautiful aerodynamic 2-seater body. Other British entries included the David Brown Aston Martin DB2 2·6-litre saloons, a make that had appeared many times at Le Mans over the years and whose entries were aimed at victory in the 3-litre class, two Cadillac-powered Allards entered by Sidney Allard and a Nash-powered Healey. In 1950 American Briggs Cunningham had entered at Le Mans two modified Cadillacs, but for the first time he was entering a team of his own cars and for the first time since the 'twenties American cars were making a serious challenge for victory. The Cunninghams were well constructed but rather cumbersome cars with 5·4-litre Chrysler engines.

A total of nine Ferraris were entered, but none of these were works cars. Although the race was led in the early laps by the Talbot of Froilan Gonzalez, by quarter-distance the Jaguar of Peter Whitehead and Peter Walker had a substantial lead, a lead that was not lost and the winner's race average of 93·495 mph was nearly 4 mph above the previous record. A Talbot was second and the Aston Martin of Lance Macklin and Eric Thompson took an excellent third place. Misfortunes struck Cunningham's gallant entries, for two crashed and the third, holding second place at half-distance, went into a sandbank and thereafter ran slower and slower until it had dropped to the tail of the field.

Cunningham had the enthusiasm and the money to return to Le Mans once more in 1952 with three cars. Mercedes-Benz had made a come-back with three very advanced cars known as the 300SL. This was based on the single overhead camshaft 3-litre Mercedes 300S touring car unit, but the engine had been extensively tuned and installed in a low aerodynamic coupé with a tubular frame, independent suspension front and rear and gull-wing doors. Mercedes even tried out in practice a car fitted with an air-brake on the roof. Panicked by the strength of the German opposition, Jaguar fitted their cars with streamlined snouts to improve air penetration, but, alas, there had been insufficient time for testing, and the Coventry cars were eliminated early in the race by overheating. With the 4·1-litre Ferraris eliminated by transmission trouble, the Mercedes sat comfortably in second and third places behind Levegh's Talbot waiting for something to break. Levegh had foolishly determined to drive through the race single-handed and he held a secure lead until the twenty-first hour of the race, when his tiredness caused him to over-rev, putting a connecting rod through the side of the engine. Levegh's drive caused him to be hailed by the press as gallant and heroic, but in realistic terms he was a fool who threw an important victory away in an attempt to satisfy his own selfish ends.

Jaguar returned to Le Mans in 1953, their cars having reverted to their old shape, but with increased power output from the use of Weber carburettors and fitted with disc brakes. Their opposition was a most formidable array of Italian cars from Alfa Romeo, Ferrari and Lancia, together with entries from Talbot, Gordini, Allard, Cunningham and Nash. The Nash entries were the Healey-based cars that had appeared at Le Mans in previous years, but as in 1952 they were prepared and entered by the American Nash works. Jaguar were intent on erasing the errors of 1952, their cars were superbly prepared and exhaustively tested, and their combination of speed and reliability annihilated the opposition; their victory was complete with works cars in first, second and fourth positions and a privately entered car ninth – the Italian failure was bitter with the retirement of the complete Alfa Romeo and Lancia teams and the sole Italian finisher was a Ferrari in fifth place. American entries fared well as the complete Cunningham team finished, in third, seventh and tenth places and a Nash-Healey was eleventh.

Ferrari returned to Le Mans in 1954 with 4·9-litre cars that appeared monstrous alongside the aerodynamically perfect and almost delicate looking new D-type Jaguars. Ferrari won and Jaguar was second. Cunninghams were third and fifth. 1955 – and the battle was renewed, but with the presence of a team of Mercedes-Benz 300SLRs that mechanically were almost identical to the Stuttgart Company's Grand Prix cars. The Mercedes were well in control of the race and made more than a match for the Jaguars and Ferraris, when Levegh's car, the Levegh of the 1952 race and Talbot fame, left the course and crashed with fatal results for the drivers and many spectators. High-level talks with the Mercedes factory in Stuttgart resulted in the withdrawal of the German cars and a hollow victory for Jaguar, a victory repeated by a privately entered Ecurie Ecosse car in 1956 and 1957. In 1956 major changes to the pits and spectator enclosures had taken place to prevent a recurrence of the previous year's disaster, the race was held in August to give time for the work at the circuit and the capacity of prototype cars was limited to 2½-litres – the D-type Jaguar was a production car by this time.

The first of a long run of Ferrari victories came in 1958 and the make won every race until 1966 apart from the 1959 event. It was in that year that the Aston Martin of Carroll Shelby and Roy Salvadori scored a well-deserved win in the race. Since 1949 David Brown, the owner of Aston Martin and Lagonda, had made regular entries with cars powered by developments of the twin overhead camshaft engine designed by W. O. Bentley for his post-war Lagonda touring car. The Aston Martin DB2 saloons had been regular winners of the 3-litre class in the early 'fifties and the DB3S sports/racing car was second in 1955, 1956 and 1958. The DBR1 that won the race in 1959 was among the fastest sports/racing cars of its time and its successes in 1959 gave Aston Martin the Sports Car Championship.

Ferrari's entries at Le Mans in the late 'fifties were beautifully executed cars of conventional design and with four overhead camshaft engines. In 1961, however, he entered a V-6 car with rear-mounted engine and that is where this story really begins. . .

TWO
The Growth of Ferrari Power

Enzo Ferrari's Early Days

To appreciate Enzo Ferrari's greatness it is necessary to know something of his background. Humble beginnings is an over-used and outdated expression, but it describes admirably Ferrari's early days. To attain his present position has not only required great ability, but a single-minded ambition bordering on ruthlessness. Enzo Ferrari was born on 18th February, 1898 at Modena and his father ran a small business supplying ironwork to the local railway. Ferrari's childhood followed a conventional enough and mundane pattern in happy family surroundings, but he took less interest in his schoolwork than in his pet pigeons. This happy pattern was sharply broken in 1916 by the death of his father from pneumonia and of his only brother, Alfredo. A year later Ferrari was conscripted into the army, but after a serious illness was discharged in 1918.

Although not as yet addicted to motor racing, Enzo Ferrari was sufficiently interested in cars to seek a job in the motor business; but, at this time, there were few jobs and many ex-servicemen desperately seeking employment. After several unsuccessful applications for jobs, Ferrari eventually found work in Turin with a back-street mechanic who specialised in stripping the bodies off light commercial vehicles and selling the chassis to coachbuilders for them to fit car bodies – a lucrative, but short-lived business in the post-World War One car boom. From Turin Ferrari moved to Milan where he worked for a small motor manufacturer, CMN (Costruzioni Meccaniche Nazionali). As a small fish in the big pool of motor car manufacturing, CMN's chances of survival were slight indeed and Ferrari naturally kept his eyes open for a more stable job. Under the guidance of Ugo Sivocci, who drove for CMN in competitions, Ferrari learnt a great deal about driving cars, handling them under difficult conditions and cornering techniques. At the age of twenty-one Ferrari was given his first big chance by CMN with a drive in the Parma Poggio di Bercetto Hill Climb and he took a creditable fourth place in this difficult and mountainous event. Later in the year CMN entered Ferrari in the Targa Florio, held as a Formula Libre race over the stone-strewn and bandit-ridden roads of Sicily. Mechanical delays dropped him to the tail of the field, but the mechanical carnage was such that he was classified ninth, despite arriving at the finish after the timekeepers had gone home!

The Start of a Long Relationship

1920 saw Ferrari find and take the opportunity he had been looking for – a job with Alfa Romeo of Milan, destined to become one of the most important motor manufacturers and to be at the forefront of Italian motor racing. Ferrari soon appeared at the wheel of a works Alfa Romeo, but although he drove competently and keenly, he lacked the stamina – a result of his earlier illness – for long distance racing and on a number of occasions ill-health prevented him from taking the wheel.

Ferrari's first major drive for Alfa Romeo was in the 1920 Targa Florio where he handled a $4\frac{1}{4}$-litre car, basically a pre-war design by Alfa's original Chief Designer Giuseppe Merosi who had been with the Company since 1910. In the Sicilian race Ferrari took an excellent second place to the Nazzaro of Meregalli, a car designed and built by former racing driver Felice Nazzaro. The following year he took second place in the Circuit of Mugello, but his most memorable race, however, was without doubt the Circuit of Savio held at Ravenna in 1923. Besides scoring his first victory for Alfa Romeo, Ferrari was presented with the now legendary 'Prancing Horse' shield by the parents of Francesco Baracca, an ace fighter pilot whose emblem it was until his death at the end of the First World War. The 'Prancing Horse' was seen on Scuderia Ferrari Alfa Romeos during the 'thirties and has appeared on Ferrari's own products ever since. In 1924 Ferrari won the Coppa Acerbo held at Pescara and scored further victories at Modena in 1927 and 1928.

At this time Nicola Romeo, who had assumed control of the Milan company during the first World War, was anxious to improve the company's status and sales and considered that the best way of doing this was by appealing to the Italian sporting instinct – through racing successes. Grand Prix racing in the early 'twenties was dominated by the Fiat concern of Turin who had a racing history dating back to the turn of the century. Alfa Romeo, on the other hand, were racing modified versions of basically production cars and if they were to challenge Fiat supremacy, advanced thinking and new designs were required from Guiseppe Merosi and the racing and sales manager Giorgio Rimini. Ferrari's role with Alfa was very much in the 'chief-bottle-washer' category and he helped with development and testing as well as working on the racing side. Ferrari was a persuasive and charming sort of fellow and having convinced Nicola Romeo that Alfas should do some poaching of engineering staff from Fiat, he went off to Turin and captured Luigi Bazzi. Bazzi was very willing to join Alfa, as he had had a disagreement with Fornaca, Fiat's chief engineer, after the 1923 French Grand Prix at Tours. Bazzi never became a significant figure at Alfa and probably is best known for the Alfa Romeo Bi-Motore cars which he designed for Scuderia Ferrari for the 1935 season; these were twin-engined racing cars with a maximum speed of 200 mph, appalling handling and a voracious appetite for tyres.

At Milan, Bazzi's first task was to assist Merosi in completing the design of the 6-cylinder P1 Grand Prix car which aped the design of the successful Grand Prix Fiat of 1922. Alfa Romeo had the cars ready in time for the 1923 Italian Grand Prix at Monza. Tragedy struck in practice for the race when Ugo Sivocci, driving one of the three cars entered, was killed in a crash. The cars were withdrawn from the race and less than a month later Ferrari, at Bazzi's suggestion, paid a visit to a flat on the third floor of a house in the Via San Massimo at Turin – a flat occupied by Vittorio Jano and his wife, Rosina. Her husband was not at home and when Ferrari told her of the reason for his call, Rosina said that her husband was too much of a Piedmontese ever to leave Turin (Turin is situated in the province of Piedmont). Jano himself arrived home shortly afterwards, settled down for a chat with Ferrari and the following day signed a contract with Alfa Romeo.

Vittorio Jano played a major role in the story of Enzo Ferrari and his background is important and of interest. He was born in 1891 at Turin, where his father was Chief of the Arsenal. After working as a technical draughtsman with a small company known as Societa Torinese Automobili Rapid, he joined Fiat in the spring of 1911 and remained with them until 1923, by when he was chief of the racing department. Jano was truly one of the greatest automobile engineers of all time – at Milan, Nicola Romeo gave him the chance to make use of his genius and to take the credit for it. Not surprisingly, Guiseppe Merosi took it badly when a younger man was brought in over his head and he left Alfa Romeo in something of a huff to join the French Mathis company.

Jano immediately set to work on a new Grand Prix design, the famous P2 with a straight eight twin overhead camshaft 2-litre engine that dominated Grand Prix racing during the years 1924 and 1925. Its impact on racing was such that Fiat withdrew from racing in the middle of the 1924 season, as their clash with Alfa Romeo in the European Grand Prix at Lyons revealed that despite an increased power output the Torinese cars were outclassed. Enzo Ferrari was entered to drive one of the P2s at Lyons, but his ill-health caused him to non-start.

For 1926 a new Grand Prix Formula limiting engine size to $1\frac{1}{2}$-litres was adopted rendering the P2s ineligible. The factory henceforth raced Jano-designed sports cars which scored a very large number of wins during 1928 and 1929. The demands of the racing department on the company's resources were becoming enormous and, in addition, it had to cope with the preparation of cars for private owners. As a result, Alfa Romeo took the tremendously important and beneficial step of placing the responsibility of racing their cars outside the factory. The man chosen was Enzo Ferrari and on 1st December, 1929, Scuderia Ferrari was formed with premises at Modena. Ferrari took over all Alfa Romeo's racing equipment and certain of their technical staff were transferred to him. While one wing of the new two-storey building in the Via Emilia was used for the preparation of the Scuderia's own competition cars, the other was devoted to the preparation and maintenance of the competition Alfa Romeos belonging to private owners.

Scuderia Ferrari

For its first year of activity Scuderia Ferrari devoted itself to sports cars and the old P2 model, two of which had been rebuilt by the works for the 1930 season. Vittorio Jano, however, was working on a new car of very advanced and sophisticated design which would be raced in both sports and Grand Prix forms and would be sold in small numbers for normal road use. This was the famous 8C-2300 model with, once again, a straight eight engine, but cast in two blocks of four cylinders and with the gear train driving the twin overhead camshafts mounted between them. The cars were superbly made and survivors of them are regarded as invaluable treasures. It was Italy's most famous road race, the Mille Miglia forming a circuit round Italy from Brescia to Rome and then back to Brescia that the new model first appeared. In this race the sports 8C Alfas were driven by Tazio Nuvolari and Luigi Arcangeli; both had crashes, but nevertheless, Nuvolari succeeded in finishing ninth. Two months later the racing version made its debut in the Italian Grand Prix at Monza. The new model, subsequently known as the 'Monza', took first and second places in this ten hour race and for the rest of this season and the early part of the next, Grand Prix racing saw exciting duels between the Monzas entered by Scuderia Ferrari, the Maseratis built at Bologna and the superbly designed and constructed Type 51 Bugattis built by Ettore Bugatti in his works at Molsheim in Alsace.

Vittorio Jano, however, had not been resting on his laurels and in 1932 there made its debut, again in the Italian Grand Prix at Monza, a further new Grand Prix car, based on the same concept as the 8C-2300, but with the larger capacity of 2·6-litres and a considerably greater power output. The new model, known as the Monoposto because of its single-seater bodywork (the Monza was a 2-seater) dominated racing throughout 1932 with consummate ease. By 1933 it became known that Alfa Romeo were in severe financial difficulties and the concern reluctantly withdrew their support from racing. This meant that the Monopostos were no longer available to Scuderia Ferrari and the team was forced to run once again the Monzas which were no real match for the improved Maseratis. Throughout the 'thirties Ferrari engaged the finest Continental drivers and all the great Italian names of the period, Varzi, Campari, Borzacchini, Nuvolari and others, raced for him at some time. The Scuderia Ferrari team was always well organised by the standards of the time and some of the great individualists rebelled against what they regarded as excessively severe team discipline. For this reason Nuvolari joined Maserati for 1933 and his driving ability was such, like that of Moss in later years, that he was more than a match for any of his compatriots even when they drove superior cars. But the Monzas were not superior, despite having engines enlarged to 2·6-litres and the fitting of carburettors made by Ferrari's great friend Edoardo Weber instead of the usual Memini instruments.

Defeat at the hands of Maserati caused Alfa Romeo to relent in the middle of the 1933 season and the Monopostos were, once again, released to the Scuderia. Until 1938 Ferrari continued to represent the Milan works in the racing field, but with depressingly less and less success. The fault was certainly not Enzo Ferrari's but the appearance for 1934 of a new Formula limiting cars by weight only and the entry into racing of two very powerful German teams, Auto Union and Mercedes-Benz. The German cars were exceedingly fast, superlatively prepared, the teams were efficiently organised and the drivers were among the best available. Scuderia Ferrari vainly raced their outdated Alfas, scoring the occasional victory when Nuvolari, who rejoined the team for 1935, outdrove or out-witted the opposition. New Alfa Romeo models appeared in 1935 and 1936, but they were still no match for the German cars.

1937 saw the departure from Alfa Romeos of Vittorio Jano who returned to Turin where he became chief engineer at Lancia. This was not, however, the end of the business relationship between him and Ferrari, as their paths were to cross yet again. 1938 brought a new Formula and a transfer of interest by Alfa Romeo from Grand Prix to voiturette racing. The cars to suit the new Grand Prix Formula were designed by Gioacchino Colombo and the responsibility for racing them was taken away from Scuderia and placed in the hands of a new organisation formed at the works and known as 'Alfa Corse'. Ferrari's ties with Alfa Romeo were still close and nominally holding the appointment of racing manager, he collaborated with Colombo in the design of a new and brilliantly successful racing car, the Tipo 158 'voiturette', which appeared in 1938. His relations with Alfa Romeo were, however, abruptly terminated in 1939. The cause was a series of violent disagreements between Ferrari and Wilfredo Ricart, a Spaniard who had been given overall control of the racing department. Ricart and Ferrari could agree on nothing, disliked each other intensely and were quite unable to work together. Certainly Ricart had his eccentricities, but Ferrari is an intolerant man and made no allowance for the Spaniard's shortcomings. Ricart continued racing development at Alfa Romeo after Italy had entered the war and was eventually forced to leave the Company by Fascist pressure.

* * *

The First Ferrari Cars

When Ferrari had been forced to give up racing the works cars under the Scuderia Ferrari banner, he entered into a severance agreement which prevented him from reconstituting Scuderia Ferrari or entering motoring competitions for a period of four years. To circumvent this difficulty his first cars were made by a concern known as Auto Avio Costruzioni and were built to compete in the 1940 Brescia Grand Prix. This race was held as a substitute for the Mille Miglia over nine laps of a 100-mile closed circuit between Brescia, Cremona and Mantua. The new car was designed by Alberto Massimino, also a former Alfa Romeo employee, and was based on Fiat components partly because they were easy to obtain and partly because the Turin company was offering a substantial award to any class winner using a Fiat-based car. The two cars were driven by the young Alberto Ascari, partnered by Giovanni Minozzi, who led the $1\frac{1}{2}$-litre class on the first lap, but retired with engine trouble, and the Marquis Rangoni, partnered by Enrico Nardi, who took the lead in the class only to be eliminated by a broken timing chain. Ascari was to become one of Ferrari's leading drivers in post-war days, but Rangoni was killed during the war. The car driven by Rangoni has survived and is in a private collection in Italy.

During the war years Ferrari was in the machine tool business. His works were transferred from Modena to a site at Maranello near the present Ferrari factory in 1943 as a result of a government attempt to decentralise industry. The new Ferrari works were bombed in both November, 1944 and February 1945, but this did not delay in any way Ferrari's efforts to be ready to re-enter racing once post-war conditions permitted. To design the new Ferrari he obtained the services of Gioacchino Colombo with whom he had closely collaborated in pre-war days. Like Jano, Colombo has proved himself to be one of the truly great Italian designers and as dramatic as was his design for Ferrari, he later substantiated his ability with the much more straight-forward, but equally successful, Maserati 250F Grand Prix car of 1954 onwards and the very unconventional Bugatti Type 251 which ran in the 1956 French Grand Prix. This featured an in-line eight cylinder engine mounted transversely at the rear of the chassis and rigid de Dion axles front and rear. The result was a very short, very wide car which on its only race appearance failed to run well. The Bugatti concern, however, lacked the money to develop the car and its true worth was never seen.

For the new Ferrari, Colombo produced a complex and high-revving, but utterly reliable 60-degree V-12 engine of largely light alloy construction with a single overhead camshaft per bank of cylinders and a seven-bearing crankshaft. In its original, unsupercharged form this had a capacity of 1498 cc (55×52·5 mm) and developed 118 bhp at 6500 rpm. In supercharged and, later, four overhead camshaft form it powered Ferrari's Grand Prix cars from 1948 until 1950. This engine was mated to a single dry-plate clutch and 5-speed gearbox and was mounted in a simple tubular chassis. The front suspension was independent by double wishbones and a transverse leaf spring, while the rigid axle at the rear also used a transverse spring as a suspension medium. With a full-width body that was sleek and aerodynamic by early post-war standards, but bulbous and cumbersome to today's eyes, the Tipo 125 *Sport* made its debut in the hands of Franco Cortese at Piacenza in 1947. Fuel pump failure caused the retirement of the Ferrari two laps from the finish, but it subsequently scored three wins in 1947 Italian sports car races.

For 1948 the Federation Internationale de l'Automobile introduced Formula Two racing for cars of up to 2000 cc unsupercharged and 500 cc supercharged, and Ferrari enlarged the capacity of his V-12 engine to comply with this new racing car Formula. The enlarged engine was also used in his sports cars. Cylinder capacity was now 1995 cc (60×58·8 mm) and with the aid of three Weber carburettors instead of the single instrument used previously, power output was boosted to 140 bhp at 6600 rpm. There were no chassis changes of an important nature, but the new sports model, designated the Tipo 166, was clad in a body by Superleggera Touring that was to be recognised as a classic of its type. Its superbly proportioned lines were subsequently imitated by both the Cooper and Tojeiro concerns in Britain and there was more than a passing similarity between the Superleggera design and the prototype A.C. Ace of 1953. This, the fastest version of the 2-litre sports Ferrari, was known as the '*Mille Miglia*', an event it won in both 1948 and 1949, but there was also offered the '*Sport*' and '*Inter*' with 89 and 110 bhp engines respectively and intended primarily for road use. The '*Mille Miglia*' with its starkly trimmed and lightly panelled body weighed a mere 12 cwt and had a maximum speed of close to 140 mph.

1949 saw the first Le Mans 24-hour race since the war and an easy victory for Luigi Chinetti and Lord Selsdon at the wheel of a '*Mille Miglia*' at an average speed of 82·27 mph. In this race the Ferrari's chief opposition came from larger capacity French sports cars of pre-war design and the 166 could truly be described as the only modern car competing at that time in sports car racing; it must be acknowledged, however, that the advantages of the Ferrari lay primarily in engine and transmission rather than chassis design. A further victory in 1949 was gained in the Belgian 24-hour Touring Car Grand Prix. The winner was again Chinetti, but partnered on this occasion by Lucas. Chinetti is now American concessionaire for Ferraris and is the sponsor of the very successful 'North American Racing Team'.

In accordance with his original plan, Ferrari progressively increased the engine capacity and there appeared 2·3-, 2·5- and 2·7-litre versions of the original sports car design. These cars did not achieve a great deal of competition success, as Ferrari's activities were split between Grand Prix and sports car racing as well as the production of road versions of his sports car for sale in the United States and Europe.

At this time, 1950, Ferrari was still racing in Grand Prix events the 1½-litre supercharged cars which were no match for the Alfa Romeo 158 designed by Colombo in pre-war days. To achieve domination in racing was the aim and if Colombo could not achieve the desired ends, then Ferrari had to replace him with a man who could. He chose Aurelio Lampredi who had been responsible for the design of the Isotta Fraschini 'Monterosa', a V-8 3½-litre rear-engined car inspired by the Czechoslovakian Tatra. The Isotta concern had found themselves in financial difficulties and the car had failed to enter production. It was decided to challenge the Alfa Romeos with an unsupercharged car based on the existing V-12 design and so the Ferrari engine was progressively increased in size during 1950, first to 3322 cc, then 4101 cc and finally, to a full 4498 cc. All these engines were used in sports/racing cars with varying degrees of success, but it was not until 1953 that Ferrari, for the first time, took the Le Mans race seriously and entered a full and well prepared team. Up until then he had been more interested in the Mille Miglia race which Ferraris won in 1950, 1951, 1952 and 1953. 1953, however, saw the introduction of a Sports Car World Championship and Ferrari was anxious to win this. Furthermore he now had sufficient staff and a clear domination of Grand Prix racing that permitted him to split his resources in this way. There is no doubt that at this time Scuderia Ferrari had attained a stage in engine development that far exceeded their ability in chassis design. All the very large Ferrari sports cars of this period had atrocious handling and required exceptional skill to drive fast and safely.

The chassis of the cars entered were identical in most respects to those of the Grand Prix cars which had overcome the 158 Alfa Romeos during the 1951 season, except that whereas the Grand Prix cars had de Dion rear axles, the sports models had a traditional rigid rear axle. Two of the cars had 4·1 litre engines, whereas that driven by World Champion Alberto Ascari and Luigi Villoresi had an engine of 4·5-litres. Each of the cars were clothed in a superbly styled coupé body of perfect proportions and an appropriately ferocious appearance designed and built by the famous coach-building firm of Pinin Farina. Although these stark beasts were probably the most powerful cars to have raced at Le Mans, they faced stiff opposition from the Jaguars which had won the race in 1951 as well as two National rivals. Alfa Romeo, having withdrawn from Grands Prix at the end of 1951, continued to race sports cars, heavily louvred and pugnacious looking 3·5-litre coupés, one of which driven by Fangio had so nearly defeated the Ferraris in the Mille Miglia. A newcomer to Le Mans was the Scuderia Lancia with superbly made 2·7-litre V-6 supercharged coupés – designed by Vittorio Jano. The race resolved itself into a duel between the Ferrari of Ascari and Villoresi and the works Jaguars. Although the Ferrari was faster, it was troubled for much of its race by a failing clutch and eventually retired on the Sunday morning. With wins in the Mille Miglia, at Spa and the Nurbürgring Ferrari secured the Sports Car Championship from Jaguar with 27 points to the Coventry team's 24.

1954 saw Enzo Ferrari racing a proliferation of different types, a tribute to the versatility of Lampredi. In the slower events over more difficult circuits, he raced 3-litre V-12 cars with better handling characteristics than their larger capacity stable mates, while a monstrous development of the previous year's Le Mans cars, a 4·9-litre car with a power output of 340 bhp and a maximum speed of close to 200 mph under favourable conditions, ran in the Mille Miglia, at Le Mans and in the Panamericana Mexico, a road race across

Above: The sole surviving and damaged Bentley makes a pit stop on the Sunday morning of the 1927 race. *Below:* The 3-litre French Ariès, driven by Chassagne and Laly, which so nearly won the 1927 Le Mans event

Above: The winning 2·3-litre Alfa Romeo about to cross the finishing line. At the wheel is Tim Birkin, while an exultant Earl Howe, his co-driver, is at the side of the road. *Below:* The winning Ferrari in the 1949 Le Mans race, the first post-war event, was a privately-entered Tipo 166 Mille Miglia 2-litre model driven by Luigi Chinetti and Lord Selsdon. Chinetti is now the American Ferrari distributor and sponsor of the N.A.R.T. team

Mexico. In addition to the V-12 models, Lampredi had produced a 4-cylinder 2-litre car with an engine and chassis similar to the previous year's Grand Prix car and intended for production. There was also a 4-cylinder 3-litre car, but this was still very much in the experimental stage.

The Mille Miglia revealed what uncontrollable beasts the 4·9-litre cars were, and both crashed. The billiard-table smooth surface and gentle curves of Le Mans were far better suited to their battleship characteristics and the race provided another clash between Ferrari and Jaguar. Two of the Ferraris were eliminated by gearbox trouble and the third, driven by Argentinian Froilan Gonzalez, whose physical proportions matched the car, and the dapper Frenchman, Maurice Trintignant scored a victory by less than a lap's lead over the D-type Jaguar of Tony Rolt and Duncan Hamilton. Towards the end of the race Trintignant pulled into the pits to hand over to Gonzalez, but the car refused to restart – a combination of damp electrics and a failing battery. The Ferrari mechanics sorted out the trouble very quickly, but by the time Gonzalez drove away from the pits, three rules had been broken: more than the permitted number of mechanics had worked on the car; the self-starter was not used to restart the car; and work was carried out with the engine running (the soft plugs used to start the engine were replaced by racing plugs). The Ferrari should have been disqualified immediately, but no action was taken by the race officials – Bill Lyons of Jaguar did not lodge an objection as it was his view that the onus was on the officials to enforce their own rules. Ferrari once again won the Sports Car Championship on the strength of wins at Buenos Aires, Le Mans and the Mexican race.

1955 was a dismal year in both Grand Prix and Sports car racing for Ferrari, as Mercedes-Benz continued their 1954 domination of the single-seater events, but were also competing in sports car races as well. At Le Mans in 1955 he fielded three new 6-cylinder 4·4-litre cars designed by Aurelio Lampredi, but although that of Castellotti led the race at the end of the first hour, all three were eliminated by overheating. In neither field of racing was Lampredi able to produce a serious challenge to Mercedes, but suddenly the problem was taken out of Ferrari's hands.

The Lancia concern of Turin had re-entered racing seriously in 1953 with sports/racing cars following the same basic concept as their production Aurelia model. In late 1954 there appeared the long awaited Lancia Grand Prix car and contracted to drive it were Alberto Ascari, the 1953 World Champion at the wheel of a Ferrari, and his team-mate and life-long friend, Luigi Villoresi. All these Lancias were the work of Vittorio Jano and the Grand Prix car was an immensely powerful V-8 of exceptionally compact dimensions. On its debut at the 1954 Spanish Grand Prix, Ascari made fastest lap in practice, with a time bettering even the Mercedes of Fangio and led the race until forced to retire with clutch trouble. The cars did not again race until 1955 when they again showed tremendous speed, but lacked reliability. In the Monaco Grand Prix, Ascari was leading the race, when a brake locked and the car plunged into Monte Carlo harbour. Ascari was apparently none the worse for his ducking apart from a fractured nose and was anxious to regain his confidence at the wheel as soon as possible. The following Thursday despite medical advice, he turned up at the Monza track where Eugenio Castellotti, another member of the Lancia Grand Prix team, was practising with a 3-litre Ferrari. At the lunchtime break Ascari asked if he could take the wheel. On the second lap the car left the road at a slight bend that could be taken almost flat out and Ascari was killed. There was no logical explanation for this accident, no sound theory, apart from Enzo Ferrari's own that Ascari had suffered a sudden embolism.

Alberto Ascari, then at the peak of his career, was the hero of Italian sport and his death shocked the Nation. As a mark of respect Lancia withdrew from racing – it must be admitted, however that they would shortly have been forced to withdraw in any case, as they were in serious financial difficulties and their competition programme had cost far greater sums than anticipated. A complete team of the World's finest Grand Prix cars were now standing unused, while Ferrari and Maserati battled in vain to defeat the might of Mercedes-Benz. The vast Fiat organisation stepped into the breach, the cars were presented to Ferrari who henceforth raced them under his own name, and Fiat provided him with a subsidy which he has had ever since. As well as receiving the cars, Ferrari took over all the racing equipment and the services of their staff who included his erstwhile colleagues Vittorio Jano and Alberto Massimino. The services of Aurelio Lampredi were now superfluous and he moved on to Fiat where he had to content himself with designing touring cars.

Ferrari raced, and as he raced them, modified the Lancia Grand

Prix cars, but as far as sports cars were concerned he reverted to the familiar V-12 layout. The 1956 Mille Miglia saw the appearance of a new model with a twin plug cylinder head and a year later Ferrari introduced a much improved car with four overhead camshafts. Although he secured the Sports Car World Championship in both 1956 and 1957, he was facing stiff opposition from Jaguar, Maserati and Aston Martin. Jaguars entered by the Scottish Ecurie Ecosse team won at Le Mans in both years.

For 1958 the Sports Car Championship was limited to cars of 3-litre capacity and Ferrari was ready with a new model which formed the basis of both his touring and sports/racing cars. The sports model was the V-12 'Testa Rossa' or red head, so called because the cylinder heads were painted red. The Testa Rossa was the mainstay of Ferrari's sports car efforts for three seasons, it first appeared in 1957 and was still being raced in certain events by the works in 1961. It was probably the best balanced and best handling of all front-engined Ferrari sports cars and quite a number of these cars were sold to private owners. It was with this model that Ferrari won at Le Mans in 1958, 1960 and 1961. The engine of the Testa Rossa was a 2953 cc ($73 \times 58 \cdot 8$ mm) unit developing upward of 300 bhp at 7200 rpm and was a tuned-up version of that used in Ferrari's 250GT road-going car. The 250GT first entered production in 1956 and it was with this model that Ferrari first made an indentation into the luxury high performance market and became recognised as a serious car manufacturer as well as racing entrant.

THREE
The Modern Ferrari

The Development of the Rear-Engined Ferrari

By 1960 Ferrari had achieved the position of being the World's most esteemed manufacturer of high-grade, high performance cars; with the withdrawal from racing of the Aston Martin sports car team at the end of the 1959 season, he was unchallenged in sports car racing and although his record of consistency in the Grand Prix field was second to none, his domination of this category had been severely shaken by British constructors. Firstly by Tony Vandervell's Vanwalls which won the Manufacturers' Championship in 1958 and secondly by the Cooper-Climax. When John Cooper's cars first appeared in Grand Prix racing in 1957, it was very much a case of John Cooper being the only man in step – all other designs raced in Formula One events at the time were front-engined, but since 1946 Coopers had been building rear-engined cars. At first these were 500 cc motor-cycle-engine-powered single seaters, but Cooper progressed to sports cars and when a 1500 cc Formula Two was introduced for 1957, built Coventry-Climax-powered racing cars to comply with it.

At first Coopers were entered in 1957 Grands Prix with the Climax engine increased in size to only 1800 cc. They were vastly underpowered compared with their rivals and were regarded as something of a joke. There had been previous rear-engined Grand Prix cars, notably the pre-war Auto Unions which were immensely powerful and difficult to control, but it had long been accepted that the conventional layout of front-mounted engine and rear wheel drive was best from the point of view of both handling characteristics and transmitting the power to the road. When Coopers won both the Argentine and Monaco Grands Prix in 1958, the successes were regarded as lucky breaks which were unlikely to recur; 1959, however, saw Jack Brabham win the Drivers' World Championship at the wheel of a Cooper with an engine of a full 2500 cc. After Brabham's early performances in the 1959 season, the other constructors realised that some drastic re-thinking about their designs was necessary and all three of the other leading contenders, BRM, Lotus and Ferrari built rear-engined cars for the 1960 season.

A major advantage of the rear-engined layout was the reduction in weight by combining the entire transmission in a single unit with the engine, and by eliminating the prop-shaft and the de Dion axle layout used on the majority of cars. Prior to the appearance of the rear-engined cars, frontal area was limited by the height of the engine. Reductions could be achieved by canting the engine, but once it was transferred to the rear, the front of the car could be lowered considerably and the driving seat dropped and angled to give a semi-recumbent position. Another advantage of the rear-engined car was that apart from concentrating the bulk of the weight where it was wanted – at the part of the car where the power was transmitted to the road – the weight distribution remained substantially unchanged as the fuel in the tanks was used up during a race. This was because the fuel tanks could be accommodated on either side of the cockpit in a rear-engined car, an arrangement that did not work well on front engined cars, because the presence of both side tanks and the transmission line made the car excessively wide.

With an increase in weight on the rear wheels from the possible maximum of 55 per cent with a front-engined car to 60 per cent on a rear-engined, it could be anticipated that the rear-engined car would oversteer violently, but this was overcome by a suitable suspension design. Indeed suspension design was the crucial factor in the design of the rear-engined Grand Prix car. With Cooper it had been a matter of luck – they just happened to build a car that handled well. Colin Chapman and the BRM Organisation employed scientific techniques in their suspension design and the cars raced by these teams handled extremely well.

Ferrari on the other hand was feeling in the dark. He had always built strong cars with engines generally more powerful than their rivals, but the V-6 Dino model raced during the 1958 to 1960 was no match for the British Cooper except on the fastest circuits. Ferrari knew he had to build a rear-engined car, but neither he nor Chief Engineer Carlo Chiti really appreciated how to go about it. In 1959 the Italian Scuderia Centro-Sud team had acquired two Coopers which they raced in Formula One events with Maserati engines. Ferrari had access to these cars for design study purposes and his first rear-engined car eventually made its debut in the 1960 Monaco Grand Prix where it was driven by Richie Ginther.

The general design of the chassis followed the lines of the Cooper and the power unit of the car was the same as that used in the normal Dino Grand Prix car. The V-6 Dino was the work of Vittorio Jano and was named after Enzo Ferrari's son. Dino Ferrari was the pride and joy of Enzo Ferrari's life, loved with the almost devotional obsession that an only son attracts, and given everything that his parents could provide. He worked in his father's factory until shortly before his death at the age of 24 in June, 1956 and it was at his suggestion that the V-6 layout was adopted. The rear-engined Ferrari was a solidly constructed car, whereas the British versions, notably the Lotus, were flimsy indeed and chassis fractures and suspension failures were a common occurrence. At Monaco, Ferrari pretended that the rear-engined Grand Prix car had a smaller engine, but it was in fact a full 2·5-litres. The car handled appallingly and after a vicious spin Ginther finished sixth. Ferrari did not again race the rear-engined car during 1960, but for 1961 he was ready with a full team of these cars with 1½-litre engines to meet the demands of the newly introduced Formula. The cars were a complete success and won seven out of nine races entered.

Sports Car Developments

The relationship between Grand Prix cars and their sports/racing prototype counterparts can be close and was at this time very close. Today Grand Prix cars have 3-litre unsupercharged engines, while the sports prototypes have much larger power units. In 1960–61, Cooper, Ferrari and Lotus all raced sports cars with similar engines to those used in their Formula One single-seaters. Differences between the two designs were limited in basic units to a wider chassis, nominal seating for two, a full-width body and the addition of lighting. Such were the Climax-powered Cooper Monaco which appeared in 1959 and the Lotus 19, nicknamed the 'Monte Carlo', announced a year later.

Similar lines of development were followed at the Maranello works and 1961 saw rear-engined sports cars raced in International events. Ferrari no longer led design trends, but was forced to imitate the ideas of the bright young British designers. The first of the new Ferraris was known as the 246/SP and used once again the Dino Grand Prix engine. The solitary car entered in the Sebring 12-hour race retired with broken steering, but an example shortly afterwards won the Targa Florio. The Sicilian race has always seen the elimination of a high proportion of the Ferrari entries through crashes and the winding, tortuous circuit is probably the most difficult to stay on with a really fast car. In the 1961 race the winning car was driven by two sensible level-headed young drivers, the vastly experienced Belgian, Olivier Gendebien, who had been driving works Ferraris, mainly GT cars, since 1955, and Grand Prix team-driver Wolfgang von Trips. The brilliant young German driver died tragically, later in the year, in the Italian Grand Prix, when his car was in collision with Jim Clark's Lotus. A 246/SP was third in the Nurbürgring 1000 Kilometres race and the only 246/SP entered at Le Mans was forced to retire when it ran out of fuel. The final event counting towards the Sports Car World Championship was the Pescara Four Hours race, where the sole 246/SP retired with a broken steering arm. 1961 was the last year in which the Sports Car Championship was held.

At the end of the 1961 season the racing side of the Ferrari organisation was split asunder by the greatest rumpus in Ferrari's career. Although Ferrari has had many disagreements with race organisers, relations within Scuderia Ferrari have generally been happy and smooth. It is in a sense a dictatorship and everything must be done the way Ferrari wants it done, but he has always chosen drivers and technicians, who, while capable of acting on their own initiative, were willing to work within the framework of activity which he had prescribed. In any forward-looking and efficient organisation men who cannot meet the demands of the job must be passed over in favour of those who can and this is why the changes of top design staff at Maranello have been frequent and almost merciless. Driver disputes had been few and the most notable had been in 1959 when the Frenchman Jean Behra was a team-driver. Behra was a volatile, short-tempered individualist and a very fine and experienced driver. When he joined Ferrari, he considered that he should be the team leader, always given the best car and generally preferential treatment. In the Ferrari organisation the drivers are a team and are expected to work together in the team's interests. The clash of personalities led to a violent argument at the 1959

French Grand Prix at Rheims and culminated in Behra striking team manager Tavoni.

Tavoni and Chief Engineer Carlo Chiti were among many of the principal Ferrari employees who left him at the end of the 1961. The reasons were personal, a clash of personalities not directly connected with the projects in hand, but at the time it seemed that they had dealt Ferrari a serious blow. It undoubtedly gave Ferrari a great deal of satisfaction that he managed to survive without his employees, while several of them found themselves in severe difficulties. Undoubtedly his technicians had learned a great deal at Maranello and it was not long before Ferrari ideas and Ferrari's approach to motor racing were seen in cars appearing from other Italian concerns.

Carlo Chiti and others joined a new concern known as the Automobile Turismo y Sport (ATS) and sponsored by Count Volpi who had previously raced cars under the banner of the Scuderia Serenissima di Republica Venezia. Two V-8 designs, a Grand Prix car and a sports prototype were produced, but the money ran out before either design could be made raceworthy. When the ATS project was wound up at the end of 1963, Count Volpi continued work on the sports prototype. One of these cars, now known as the Serenissima, ran without success at Le Mans in 1966 and the engine was also tried out in the 1966 McLaren Formula One car. Carlo Chiti was originally with Alfa Romeo and has now returned to that Company to run the Autodelta team of Alfa Romeo Guilia modified production cars and Tipo 33 sports prototypes. The Tipo 33 prototype has a V-8 engine and that has more than a passing similarity to the V-8 raced by Ferrari shortly after Chiti left the Maranello concern. Other Ferrari technicians joined Ferraccio Lamborghini and collaborated with him in the production of the range of Lamborghini Gran Turismo cars. These superbly constructed V-12 cars have now achieved a reputation matching that of Ferrari. Indeed the wheel has turned full circle and the latest version of the Dino 2-litre V-6 GT Ferrari has the engine mounted tranversely at the rear, a layout first seen on the 2-litre 6-cylinder Lamborghini 'Marzal' which has not yet entered production.

In the Grands Prix held during the years 1962 to 1965 Ferrari progressed from the V-6 layout through a V-8 to a flat 12. Similar lines of development were followed in the sports car field. 1962 saw the appearance of a 2½-litre V-8 rear-engined car known as the 248/SP and distinguished, as were Ferrari's Grand Prix cars of the

The winner of the 1953 race was the Jaguar XK120C of Tony Rolt and Duncan Hamilton. Rolt is seen at Arnage

The years 1953–4 saw a tremendous battle for supremacy at Le Mans between Jaguar and Ferrari. In 1953 Jaguars' chief opposition came from the very fierce 4·5-litre Ferrari coupé of Alberto Ascari and Luigi Villoresi. After harrying the Jaguars for twelve hours, the Ferrari retired with clutch trouble on the Sunday morning, but not before it had set a new lap record of 112·63 mph

time, by twin nostril air intakes. The 6-cylinder cars were still raced and as Ferrari's opposition in sports car races was largely limited to Maseratis entered by private teams and the smaller capacity Porsche works entries, he had little difficulty in dominating the sports car scene. The 246/SP won both the Targa Florio and at the Nürburgring, while an experimental V-12 4-litre car was the victor at Le Mans. Richie Ginther had left Ferrari at the end of 1961 to join the BRM team and Phil Hill also went elsewhere after 1962. With the appearance of V-8 engines from Coventry-Climax and BRM, the British cars enjoyed far greater success during 1962. Phil Hill's last season with Ferrari was none too happy and he did not succeed in winning a single Grand Prix. After ten years of driving privately owned and works Ferraris, he joined the ATS team.

For 1963 Ferrari reverted to the V-12 layout and raced the 250/P with a revised version of the 'Testa Rossa' engine and it is with derivatives of the 250/P that Ferrari has met the challenge from Ford at Le Mans and elsewhere. In this form, with six twin-choke Weber carburettors and a compression ratio of $9 \cdot 7 : 1$, the 'Testa Rossa' engine developed 310 bhp at 7500 rpm. The transmission was by a single-plate clutch and a 5-speed gearbox in unit with the final drive which incorporated a ZF limited slip differential. A multi-tubular steel chassis frame was used and the suspension, which was by double unequal length wishbones and combined coil springs and Koni dampers front and rear, was, together with the engine and other mechanical components, enclosed by a built-up superstructure. British Dunlop disc brakes were fitted on all four wheels, mounted inboard at the rear, and two master cylinders were used, giving separate brake circuits front and rear, As with the majority of Ferraris the cars were fitted with right-hand drive and Ferrari rack-and-pinion steering requiring two turns from lock-to-lock. The earliest cars were open models and had the twin nostril air intakes. Later in the year there appeared the 330/P which had a 3967 cc (77×71 mm) engine developing 400 bhp at 7500 rpm.

In the first race of the season, the Sebring 12-hour race held on the rather desolate and dull Florida airfield circuit, Ferraris completely dominated the race, taking the first six places. 250/Ps driven by John Surtees and Lovobico Scarfiotti took first and Willy Mairesse and Nino Vaccarella second places respectively. An experimental 4-litre car entered in the name of the North American Racing Team was third and Gran Turismo Ferraris occupied the next three places.

Victory in the Targa Florio went to Porsche, not surprisingly as this race favours a smaller superlatively handling car. In addition, 250/Ps won both at the Nurbürgring and at Le Mans. At this time Ferrari was virtually unbeatable in sports car racing.

Ferrari Production Methods

The Ferrari factory at Maranello is a compact, modern and efficient unit devoted solely to the production of high-performance cars and employing approximately 450 persons. The greatest possible care is taken by the workers in the assembly and construction of the cars, and much of this is done by hand. The cars leave the factory to a standard of finish unmatched by other constructors except Rolls-Royce and Lamborghini. Ferrari has his own foundry, occupying some 5000 square feet, and there he produces all the castings needed for his cars, including the magnesium and alloy castings. As late as 1954, however, Maserati were still producing the cylinder heads and blocks used by Ferrari. There is an enormous machine shop where each employee is in charge of a machine and works to very close tolerances from a drawing on the machine. After machining, every part is subjected to a crack test under ultra-violet light and other tests, where appropriate, include measuring for breaking strain and microscope testing of gear flanges. Ferrari has his own copper deposit and plating plants and even all the bolts used in the construction of the cars are heat treated.

After the chassis have been welded up, they go by lorry to the coachbuilder for the body to be fitted. The big 4-litre 330GT production model has a body by Farina of Turin while the smaller 3·3-litre 275GTB is fitted with a body by Scaglietti, but this too is styled by Farina. Although certain of the competition cars have bodies built in the Maranello works, others are the responsibility of Scaglietti whose works are conveniently situated in Modena. After their return from the coachbuilders, the body/chassis frame units enter the assembly line where the running gear, back axle, suspension and similar components are carefully and painstakingly installed.

Engine assembly is to racing standards and it takes approximately 36 hours work from two men to assemble a simple unit. Each production engine is then run in for ten hours at speeds between 1400 and 3600 rpm, for a further two hours at between 4000 and

6000 rpm and, in conclusion, a check for power output at 7000 rpm. After assembly, each car is taken out for a test run lasting up to half an hour. Despite all the labour going into the production of these cars, a rival Italian manufacturer has estimated that Ferrari's profit margin can be as much as 100 per cent.

Unlike many of his rivals, Ferrari is not secretive about what is going on in the racing department. Each year Ferrari shows his new developments to the press and visitors to Maranello are not prevented from seeing the racing department. Here the cars are built up on stands which give the best access for working on them and there is the atmosphere of a closely-knit group of men whose hearts are truly in motor racing and who would rather be engaged on this work than any other regardless of what financial rewards were offered.

The local populace has become accustomed to the sight of the factory gates swinging open and the latest sports/racing car accelerating away with a sudden deafening roar and leaving two very black, thick lines of rubber on the road surface. The red blur of a sports/racing Ferrari weaving along a narrow 20-foot road between the bicycles, the Vespa scooters and the bullock carts is an awe-inspiring sight and certainly not one to be seen outside Italy. Modena Autodrome is, of course, nearby and a great deal of serious testing takes place both there and at Monza.

Ferrari's Attitude to Racing

Since 1948 Ferrari has been engaged in both sports car and Grand Prix racing and counting Formula Two as well, he has at times been competing in three categories simultaneously. No other racing car constructor has such varied interests and there is no doubt that this diversity is a weakness. At times he has been forced to let one form of racing suffer, through concentrating on another and in the last few years his sports car battle with Ford has been conducted at the expense of Grand Prix successes. At one time Ferraris would compete in every possible event both inside and outside Italy, sometimes running in two different countries on the same day, but now Ferrari restricts his entries to the most important events only. Instead of entering six or eight cars in major sports car races, as was his practice, Ferrari now limits the number of his entries to four at the most, but ensures that the works cars are supported by entries from private owners who can afford the latest equipment and the best drivers. Among these private teams are Maranello Concessionaires Limited, the British Ferrari concessionaires, the North American Racing Team sponsored by Luigi Chinetti, the American agent, The Equipe Nationale Belge and the Swiss Scuderia Filipinetti.

Ever since he started racing under his own name with success, Ferrari realised his importance as the figure-head of Italian motor racing and the prestige that his efforts have brought to the Italian motor industry as a whole, and especially to the giant Fiat organisation. Since he was given the Lancia racing equipment in 1955, Ferrari has received large subsidies from Fiat which have gradually increased over the years. No one will breathe a word as to how much he actually receives, but there is little doubt that the sum received from Fiat is every bit as great as that pumped each year into racing by the Ford Company. In addition to the profits received from the sale of production cars, Ferrari receives very strong support from the motor trade, notably fuel and tyre companies, probably to the tune of well over £100,000. He also expects and gets substantial starting money for his works entries.

For a combination of reasons Enzo Ferrari no longer attends motor races. As a former driver himself, he has found the nervous tension rather more than he could tolerate in his older years; he does not like to see the cars so carefully prepared in his works broken up through overdriving or being crashed; and he dreads seeing his drivers hurt or killed in a crash. Enzo Ferrari is well aware of the risks his drivers take and probably more drivers have been killed in post-war days at the wheel of a Ferrari than all other makes combined. This is simply because Ferraris have been racing longer and far more consistently than other makes. Obviously Ferrari's relations with his drivers have varied according to the personality involved. Since the death of his son in 1956, he has tended to adopt a paternal attitude towards his younger drivers and his affections for Eugenio Castellotti and Luigi Musso were particularly strong. These rather wild, young Italian drivers vied with each other for the Italian Championship and were as friendly off the circuits as they fought fiercely against each other on the track. Castellotti was killed during a test run at Modena in 1957 and Musso died after a crash at Rheims the following year.

Although the Ferrari organisation is a powerful and wealthy concern, it has such a friendly atmosphere that it is almost inevitably regarded as a small family business. In Ferrari's battle with Ford, the Italian concern is often looked on as the little man tackling the full might of big business. In fact, the two teams were closely matched in terms of both technical 'know-how' and finances, but with the balance of experience in Ferrari's favour.

FOUR
The Cobra Factor

Even before Ford had entered the motor racing scene, their name was being represented on the racing circuits of the World by the Ford-powered Cobras of the small Californian concern run by former racing driver Carroll Shelby. Shelby was one of the small band of American drivers who had successfully broken into big time European motor racing and his tall, muscular figure and broad grin were a familiar sight in the late 'fifties.

All his life Shelby has only been interested in cars and flying. During the Second World War Shelby was a pilot in the Training Command and flew just about everything from Dakotas to Flying Fortresses. On one occasion he was forced to bail out over West Texas. Having made a safe landing, he set off in the dark to find help and came to a fork in the road; if he had taken the correct fork he would have had only a mile to walk to the town of Matador, but he took the other fork and walked 35 miles across the second largest ranch in the World!

After his demob, Shelby tried several different jobs, but was not really happy in any of them. He did, however, manage to take up sports car racing, at first with a slow and rather elderly MG 'TC', but graduated the following year to a very much hotter Jaguar XK120. His next car was a stark and hairy Cadillac-Allard and he ran this in the 1954 Buenos Aires 1000 kilometres race where he took tenth place. After the race John Fitch, a very experienced American driver and in 1952 a member of the works Mercedes-Benz team, offered to take him to Europe to show him the ropes of motor racing European-style. To compete in European events he acquired one of the new Aston Martin DB3S cars and ran this in American blue and white racing colours.

At Le Mans, co-driving with Belgian journalist Paul Frère, he ran his car as a member of the works team and loaned them his car on more than one occasion when the ranks of the works cars were depleted by crashes. In 1955 Shelby was in Europe again at the wheel of a fast, but fickle 6-cylinder 4·4-litre Ferrari. In 1957 he won the SCCA (Sports Car Club of America) National Championship driving a Ferrari for wealthy entrant John Edgar. The following year he was back in Europe as a member of the works Aston Martin team. At the wheel of the sports DBR1 Aston, Shelby displayed both speed and skill and his successes for the Feltham team included a win, co-driving with Roy Salvadori, in the 1959 Le Mans race. He also drove the unsuccessful Aston Martin DBR4/250 Grand Prix car, a Maserati belonging to the Scuderia Centro-Sud and a lightweight version of the same car owned by anotherwealthyAmerican enthusiast, Temple Buell.

At the end of 1960 Shelby gave up driving, because of a slight heart condition. One of his reasons for competing in Europe had been to learn as much as he could about quality European car manufacturers such as Aston Martin and Maserati and their methods and he now felt sufficiently knowledgeable to put what he had learnt into practice. It had long been his ambition to market in the USA a sports car based on a European chassis, but with all the advantages of a standard large capacity American engine – initial low costs, equally low cost and availability of spare parts. Back in 1957 he had talks with Ed Cole who was Vice-President and General Manager of the Chevrolet division of General Motors. Chevrolet were in principle willing to supply Shelby with engines, but a number of snags, including the prospective competition to their own Corvette sports car programme, cropped up and the project was dropped. It was, therefore, not until the Autumn of 1961 that Shelby made any definite moves towards marketing his own cars.

Shelby approached the AC Company of Thames Ditton to see whether they would co-operate with him. AC, founded in 1907, had been making high quality cars powered by a single overhead camshaft alloy engine first introduced in 1919 and used it in their new Ace sports model which appeared at the 1953 London Motor Show. The Ace was in fact the Tojeiro made under licence and this in turn followed closely in suspension design the Cooper sports car of the period – one of the very few Cooper designs to have a front-mounted engine. John Tojeiro, a young Englishman of Portuguese descent, had started racing in 1950 with a pre-war MG 'TA' Midget to which he had fitted a lightweight body. The rather perilous roadholding of this device led him to scrap the existing chassis and build a new one from scratch. Roughly following the lines of the pre-war Mercedes Benz Grand Prix cars, the new Tojeiro chassis was based on two large diameter steel tubes with a central tubular cross-member and steel boxes at each end carrying the suspension. The suspension was fully independent front and rear by a transverse leaf spring and lower wishbones. This chassis design formed the basis of a number of specials raced by different enthusiasts and culminated in a Bristol-powered car, with bodywork copied from the Tipo 166 'Mile Miglia' Ferrari, which Cliff Davis raced during the 1953 season.

It was this model which AC had put into production as the Ace, but with slight styling changes and powered by AC's old-fashioned engine. With its large frontal area (far greater than that, for example of the Triumph TR2) and its ancient and rather breathless engine, the Ace could just about stagger up to 100 mph, but in all other respects it was a very beautiful car. To increase performance, the Ace was offered from 1956 with the 2-litre Bristol engine developing 125 bhp in its most powerful production form. This endowed the Ace with a top speed of close to 120 mph and it became a popular model in British Club racing. A modified Ace-Bristol took second place to a Ferrari in its class at Le Mans in 1957, and a special competition version of the Ace with a Tojeiro-designed space-frame chassis won the class in the following year's race.

In 1961 the Bristol Company stopped manufacture of their 2-litre engine and started using a Chrysler unit to power their saloons. Supplies of the Bristol engine became very limited and AC then turned to the 2·6-litre Ford Zephyr engine as an alternative power unit. Although the Ford engine could be tuned to a higher degree than the Bristol, it did rather look as though the AC Company had reached the end of the road with the Ace. The company were interested in Selby's idea of fitting the Ace with the 221 cubic inch Ford engine and a Borg-Warner gearbox and the success of the project was assured when the American Ford Company agreed to supply engines. An engine and gearbox were transported from the States and installed in an Ace body/chassis unit at Thames Ditton where the preliminary testing was done in early 1962. These tests revealed the need for a number of modifications to the chassis. The chassis frame was strengthened and a longer front spring was fitted. The engine and gearbox were then removed and the car was flown to the United States for Shelby to continue its development work.

After the installation of a 260 cubic inch (4260 cc) Ford engine the car was then taken to Riverside Raceway for further testing and early changes were the fitting of a Holley carburettor and anti-roll bars front and rear (optional on the production cars). A great deal of the development work, especially that concerning the engine, and cooling of both the engine and the cockpit of the car, was carried out at the Ford works at Dearborn. The car made its first race appearance at Riverside Raceway in October, 1962 where it retired with hub failure. These were strengthened on the production cars, and the chassis tubes were increased in strength and diameter. The prototype was followed to the States by three further cars which were used for development work and one of these later formed the basis of the Ford Cougar II styling experiment.

Well satisfied with the development programme, Shelby decided to plunge in with production of his new sports car. He managed to scrape together 40,000 dollars to finance the project and for no obvious or logical reason decided to call the car the 'Cobra' – he thought the name sounded attractive, but it did not meet with unanimous approval either with dealers or buyers. In the United States, the car became known as the Ford Cobra and the original badge on the bonnet bore the name 'Shelby Cobra' with the AC emblem in the centre. Later the familiar pictorial Cobra badge was adopted. The Ford Company ensured that their contribution to the car was recognised by the fitting of 'Ford Powered' badges on the front wing panels. In addition, the cars became homologated by the Federation Internationale de l'Automobile as the Shelby American Cobra, so the AC origins of the car became rather overlooked.

Shelby succeeded in making arrangements for the Cobra to be marketed in the States through Ford dealers, but originally he was thinking in terms of marketing only the original order of 100. However, soon after finishing and final assembly work had started at Shelby's small Santa Fé works, a further hundred was ordered. Demand soon reached a level far exceeding Shelby's expectations. To cope with it AC were forced to give up making cars for the home market and Shelby moved on to larger works at Venice, also in California, formerly occupied by the Scarab sports car project of Lance Reventlow, son of Woolworth heiress Barbara Hutton. Total production amounted to about 1500 cars. The reasons for the Cobra's popularity are not difficult to see. The body and chassis were typically European in concept and the Cobra is far better looking than average. To this obvious appeal was added a performance that was vastly superior to the average European sports car and the virtually standard engine was in no way temperamental and did not require much in the way of maintenance.

At first Cobras were made only in red or white, but demand soon forced Shelby to add black, blue, green and maroon to the colour range. The first 75 cars were powered by the 260 cubic inch (4·2-litre) Ford engine, but subsequent cars have had the 289 cubic inch (4·7-litre) unit. From early in 1963, after the construction of the first 125 cars, rack-and-pinion steering was substituted for the worm-and-sector fitted at first. On the worm-and-sector steering of the early Cobras there was an excessively lengthy idler arm and two track rods to each steering arm. One result of this was that when the cars were being raced, the toe-in altered driving wheel travel. A heavy strain was then thrown on the ball joints of the idler arm with the result that the idler arm bracket failed. The standard Ford gearbox was changed in 1963 for a box with Pontiac gears which was better suited to the Cobra's engine characteristics. The most drastic change to the Cobra was made in May, 1965 when the traditional transverse leaf spring layout was scrapped in favour of the much more modern system of unequal length wishbones and combined coil spring and damper units.

It was not until 1964 that the Cobra became available on the British market and in the middle of the following year AC and Shelby American Inc. came to an arrangement whereby Shelby was to market cars in the USA with the 7-litre Ford engine only and AC were to be entirely responsible for the marketing of the 4·7-litre Cobra which for the 1965 London Motor Show was renamed the AC '289'. AC do, however, make a very luxurious version of the Cobra with a 7-litre engine. This has a wheelbase lengthened from 7 ft 6ins., to 8 ft, and is fitted with a handsome open or coupé body by the Italian coachbuilder Frua and generally very similar to that fitted by Frua to the Maserati Mistrale. AC call this model the '428', but its very high price (£3750 without purchase tax) has resulted in only a small number being made.

From its conception Shelby had intended the Cobra to be raced and had especially in mind private owners competing in the Sports

Car Club of America production class. Production competition versions of the Cobra were offered on the American market at a fixed price tag, but, as is usual, the works competition cars were rather faster than those sold to the general public. Modifications to Cobras for racing included generally tuning the engine, fitting larger valves and carburettor changes. On Shelby-entered cars the carburettors have been four down-draught Weber 48 IDM instruments. Other racing developments have included a cast aluminium sump, a special clutch housing to protect the driver from injury in the event of the clutch shattering and a special gearbox with an aluminium casing and closer ratios. Halibrand magnesium wheels, often fitted to Indianapolis cars, are the usual wear on Racing Cobras. As these are wider, it is necessary to bend the steering arms to give extra clearance – a practice reminiscent of the blacksmith's shop rather than modern racing technology.

Shelby naturally wanted to race the cars himself to gain publicity and extra sales and the encouragement and support of the Ford Company led him to embark on a far more extensive racing programme than he had originally envisaged. For, as the cars were marketed through Ford dealers and known as Ford Cobras, every success brought publicity to Fords as well as to Cobras. In addition as Fords were already preparing to challenge for honours in the prototype category of sports car racing, they saw in the Cobra a means of having a crack at the Grand Touring Championship at the same time. This Championship had been first introduced by the Federation Internationale de l'Automobile for the 1961 season.

The first important race for the Cobra was 1963 Daytona Continental Grand Touring race held in February, an event which had been inaugurated the previous year as a sports car event. Four works Cobras were fielded, but mechanical troubles dogged the team and the sole finisher was Dave McDonald in fourth place. The following month another strong entry was fielded in the Sebring 12-hours race. Sebring was an important race and one of the four counting towards the Grand Touring Championship. The Cobras displayed an impressive turn of speed, but once again lacked the reliability to match their performance. Of the four Cobras starting, the sole finisher was the car driven by Phil Hill and Ken Miles which was placed eleventh.

Although raced in many American National events during the year, the Shelby team made only one European appearance in 1963.

Shelby regarded this as an experimental year during which he would get the cars thoroughly sorted out and gain valuable experience. Part of the experiment was to run at Le Mans and two cars were entered. One of these was a car entered jointly by Ed Hugus and Shelby and driven by Hugus and the British driver Peter Jopp. The other entry was something of a publicity seeker. It was entered by the AC Company and sponsored by *The Sunday Times*. The drivers were Ninian Sanderson, who had co-driven the winning Ecurie Ecosse Jaguar in the 1956 race, and Peter Bolton who had driven AC Aces at Le Mans previously. Both entries were managed by Stirling Moss – useful publicity for Cobra and useful for Moss who was seeking experience for the running of the 'Stirling Moss Automobil Racing Team'. The race was completely dominated by Ferraris which took first six places, but, despite a rather sub-standard 'cooking' engine, the Thames Ditton Cobra was seventh home. The Shelby entry was eliminated by a broken connecting rod in the eleventh hour, but in any case would have been disqualified for taking oil too soon.

1964 was the important year in Cobra racing history, for now, with full support from Ford, Shelby made a determined effort at cracking Ferrari domination in the Grand Touring Category. Cobras ran in almost all the events counting towards the Grand Touring Championship and faced the 250GTO Ferrari, the most advanced of all Ferrari's touring car designs. This had been evolved by Vittorio Jano from the existing 250GT and had the full 'Testa Rossa' engine with six Weber carburettors and a power output of 300 bhp at 7400 rpm. A full works racing Cobra developed approximately 350 bhp at 7000 rpm. The multi-tubular steel chassis of the 250GTO was clad with a paper thin light alloy body and the whole car scaled a mere 21 cwt. The beautifully proportioned body designed by Pinin Farina and built by Fantuzzi in the Ferrari works had a delicacy of line and a grace which contrasted sharply with the stark, almost brutal lines of the Cobra. The GTO's roadholding, despite a rigid rear axle, was undoubtedly superior, and it also had the advantage of a 5-speed gearbox with synchromesh on all ratios. The two cars were however closely matched in terms of acceleration and maximum speed which was about 185 mph in both cases.

Cobra's first race of 1964 was the Daytona event, again in February, but held over a distance of 2000 kilometres instead of for three hours as previously. Initially the new Cobra Daytona coupé of Bob

Holbert and Dave McDonald built up a substantial lead over a pack of following GTO Ferraris, but it was eliminated by catching fire during a refuelling stop. This incident gave the lead and victory to the Ferrari of Phil Hill and Pedro Rodriguez. The highest placed Cobra was that of Dan Gurney and Bob Johnson in fourth place. Sebring, a month later, was another Ferrari benefit, but unlike Daytona, was for both sports prototypes and GT cars. Although the Ferrari prototypes took first three places, Shelby achieved all he had set out to do and as well as taking first three places in the GT categories, Cobras were fourth, fifth and sixth overall.

The Daytona was based on the usual AC-built chassis, but was fitted with an entirely new aerodynamic closed body with a longer and more pointed nose and a chopped tail. With its 4·7-litre engine tuned to develop close to 350 bhp, the claimed maximum speed of the Daytona was just under 200 mph. This body was designed by 27-year-old Pete Brock, who had at one time worked for the Special Vehicle Development Section of General Motors and who had carried out much of the early Cobra test driving. Shelby had planned to race a Daytona coupé with a lengthened chassis and powered by the 6·8-litre Ford Galaxie engine, but Ford had discouraged this project as the car would have been as fast as the Ford prototype coupés.

The Shelby team then moved on to their next event, the first of their European season and the most difficult. This was the Targa Florio, famed as a car-breaker both mechanically and by crashes. The winding Sicilian roads did not favour the Cobra's ponderous roadholding and Shelby knew that the chances of doing well were slight. All the Cobra drivers could hope to do was slam their accelerator foot hard down on the short straights, hear the revs. rise with a shattering bang, as they do with these Ford engines, and then stand on the brakes, gritting their teeth and hoping that the car would find its way round the next corner. All this was accompanied by a noise and vibration level that had to be experienced to be believed. Indeed it is possible to stand 8 or 10 ft away from a hot Cobra that is being 'blipped' and feel the ground vibrating under one's feet. Despite the inclusion in the team of Dan Gurney, the works Brabham Grand Prix driver, and Phil Hill, the most experienced American in European racing, and despite the absence of works Ferraris, it was not a good race for the Shelby team. Out of five cars entered, only one finished, that of Dan Gurney and Jerry Grant in eighth place, and this had broken suspension. Victory in this event did, however, go to a Grand Touring car, the 2-litre 904GTS Porsche of Pucci and Colin Davis with a similar car in second place.

Shortly afterwards Shelby ran three of the ordinary open Cobras and the Daytona coupé in the Spa 500-kilometres race for homologated Grand Touring cars. There was a good entry of privately owned GTO Ferraris, but it seemed that the Daytona coupé driven by Hill might well win. Phil Hill is never very happy on slow, 'tight' circuits, but infinitely prefers a circuit with high lap speeds and long sweeping bends. At Spa he was only fractionally slower in practice than Mike Parkes with a GTO entered by Maranello Concessionaries, but was delayed on the first lap by fuel starvation which took a long time to sort out. With lap speeds of around 125 mph, the open Cobras proved no match for the Ferraris and Mike Parkes had an easy win.

Drivers consider that the Nurbürgring in Germany is one of the most difficult circuits of all, for it is long, exceptionally hard on the suspension of the cars, the many bends require a great deal of experience and judgment to get sized up and as a comparatively slow circuit, it certainly favours the fastest drivers, as opposed to the fastest cars. It was here that the Cobras met up with the GTO Ferraris once more in May. The Shelby American entries were supported by entries from the British Willment team. This team was sponsored by John Willment, a Ford distributor and a great racing enthusiast who had previously built a Coventry-Climax-powered sports car bearing his own name. One of the Willment Cobras was eliminated in practice by a crash caused by the engine seizing up and at the start the carburettors of the other Willment car caught fire. All the Shelby entries had trouble, but nevertheless the Cobra of Jo Schlesser and Dick Attwood had an easy win in the over 3000 cc Grand Touring Category.

At Le Mans the Cobras were out in force and heading them were two of Shelby's new Daytona coupés. There were only the two because the Cobra chassis had been held up in the customs at Modena. In addition to the Shelby cars, an AC works entry was driven by Jack Sears and Peter Bolton. This car became the centre of an amusing controversy, as it was alleged that it had been driven at 183 mph on the M1 motorway during pre-Le Mans testing. There was an MoT enquiry, and Mr William Swallow, president of the Society of Motor Manufacturers and Traders was forced to give an assurance that manufacturers would not do high-speed testing on public roads again. This incident also highlighted the great increase in power output which Shelby had found in twelve months, for the maximum speed of the British entered car in the 1963 race was only 165 mph.

Le Mans with its long straight, smooth surface and comparatively easy bends was well suited to the Cobra's characteristics and, for once, the Ferrari GTOs were never really in the picture. Although Ferraris took first three places in general classification, the Shelby entry of Dan Gurney and Bob Bondurant justified all the work and money put into the Cobra's racing programme by finishing fourth and winning the GT category.

From Le Mans the Shelby team moved on to the historic city of Rheims for the 12-hour sports car race accompanying the French Grand Prix. This race was a disappointment, as the Daytona coupés of both Gurney/Bondurant and Innes Ireland/Neerpasch retired with split gearbox casings. Another Championship race well supported by Shelby was the 130-lap RAC Tourist Trophy at Goodwood where Cobras took third, fourth and fifth places overall behind Graham Hill (Ferrari 330/P) and David Piper (Ferrari 275LM). These were driven by Dan Gurney (Daytona coupé), Jack Sears and Bob Olthoff (Willment entries). Shelby did not support the Paris 1000-kilometre race at Montlhéry, but nevertheless won the 1964 Grand Touring Championship.

The Shelby Organisation is small, but despite the continual development on the production cars, the increasing demand for Cobras and Shelby's active engagement in the Ford GT project, he decided to defend his Grand Touring Championship the following season. At Daytona a coupé shared by Keck, Johnson and Schlesser took second place in general classification and the make was again the first Grand Touring car home at Sebring where Schlesser and Bondurant were fourth overall with a coupé. In the Monza 1000-kilometres race, the class-winning Cobra of Bondurant and Grant took eighth place overall, but was defeated by the 914GTS Porsche of Pon and Slotemaker which won the smaller GT category.

Cobra were now facing opposition in the Grand Touring races from a new Ferrari model, the Tipo 275GTB. This was powered by a 3·3-litre version of the usual V-12 engine and was basically a production car selling in quite large numbers. The competition versions, of course, had a full race engine with six Weber carburettors and very light coachwork. Despite this, the Daytona coupés continued to dominate their class. In the Nürburgring 1000-kilometres race the Daytonas won their class and finished sixth and tenth overall. The preparation of the entries for this were delegated to Alan Mann, who plays not an inconsiderable role in the story of the Ford GT, for Shelby was concentrating all his efforts on the Le Mans race held the following month where he was the entrant of two of the Ford GTs.

At the Sarthe circuit a grand total of five Daytonas were entered, two by Shelby American and the others by Ford-France, AC Cars and the Scuderia Filipinetti. The last three were, however, prepared by Alan Mann. Cobra fortunes were beginning to wane and only one car finished, despite tremendous pre-race promise. The only GT Ferrari entered was a 275GTB driven by Willy Mairesse and 'Beurlys' and this had insufficient speed to stay with the Cobras. Then the Cobra mechanical troubles started, two of the cars went sick and fell out during the night, while Jack Sears smashed in the front of the AC entry and resumed the race after the radiator had been changed. The remaining two Cobras were suffering from falling oil pressure and a broken crankshaft damper respectively and both retired. The lone Cobra, looking decidedly second-hand staggered on to finish eighth, whereas the steady and consistent running of the 275GTB brought it third place overall and victory in the Grand Touring Category.

With these successes, the Cobras had scored sufficient points to repeat their win in the Grand Touring Championship, but it was clear that they had reached the peak of their development. Already Shelby's works were increasingly concentrating on the production of modified high-performance versions of the Ford Mustang and for 1966 the whole concept of racing Grand Touring cars was changed. The representative of the Ford Company in this category became the production version of the Ford GT40 which raced against the rear-engined Ferrari 275LM. Despite its early demise at the forefront of racing, the role of the Cobra was important. It represented the first serious and successful attempt by an American entrant to break into European racing since the efforts of Briggs Cunningham and it was the first form of International racing to pay off for the Ford Company.

Above: At the Maranello works Mike Hawthorn is about to test on the public roads a 4·9-litre Ferrari of the type which won the 1954 Le Mans race. Standing behind the car are his father Leslie (right) with Reg Parnell next to him and Dino Ferrari second from left. *Below:* Duncan Hamilton is seen about to leave the pits in the second place Jaguar in the 1954 race

Above: American millionaire Briggs Cunningham was an enthusiastic supporter of Le Mans, both with his own cars and with Ferrari, Maserati, Osca and Jaguar entries. One of Cunningham's entries in 1953 was this 5454 c.c. Chrysler-powered car with aerodynamically efficient coupé bodywork designed by Professor Kamm. Driven by Moran and Bennett, it took tenth place. *Below:* Nash-Healeys, with a chassis designed by Donald Healey and Nash engines, ran at Le Mans in 1950-53. In 1952 and 1953 the cars were entered by the Nash Company and this car driven by Johnson and Hadley took eleventh place in 1953

FIVE
The Development of the Ford GT

The Reason Why

Just as many manufacturers, such as the Daimler-Benz Organisation and Jaguar, are expected and accepted entrants in motoring competition, others by tradition eschew all forms of racing. Until recent years the giant Ford organisation was in the latter category. The 'sixties has, however, seen a revolution in Ford thinking, and they have recently actively supported and participated in many different forms of motoring competition. Their activities have included the supply of and co-operation in the development of engines for Formula Junior, Formula Three and Formula Two racing, the development of the engines powering the Lotus works cars at Indianapolis and the operation of a full works rally team by the British Ford Company.

To gain a strong foothold in the heart of International motor racing, Fords endeavoured to buy the Ferrari organisation. Ferrari did not reject the Ford overtures out of hand, but negotiations fell through and even if Enzo Ferrari had come to satisfactory terms with Ford it is doubtful whether he would have been allowed to go through with the transaction. Of Europe's two largest motor manufacturers, Volkswagen and Fiat, it is frequently said that Germany owns Volkswagen, but Italy belongs to Fiat. Certainly Fiat financial interests in Italy are vast, but the prestige that Ferrari's activities bring to Fiat and Italy are equally vast. It is very likely that Fiat would have brought pressure to bear on the Italian government to prevent any sale of the Ferrari concern proceeding.

But why was Ford so interested in making a success of motor racing? To quote the words of Charles H. Patterson, Executive Vice-President of the Ford Company: 'Our racing programme is . . . a prudent business investment. Our product improvement and sales records can be attributed to many factors, but we have no hesitation in saying that racing is one of them' Patterson went on to enumerate four tangible advantages derived from Ford's racing activities:

1. The ordinary everyday products benefit from the development and the use of new ideas in racing. The net result of racing is a safer, more reliable, more durable, more efficient form of motor transportation, 'which is our stock-in-trade'.

2. 'When we say 'racing improves the breed', we don't just mean the mechanical aspects of our motor vehicles. We also mean it improves the breed of engineers, designers and manufacturing people who adapt these improvements for highway use. From this work on racing cars, these specialists know more about automobiles – faster and sometimes more painfully – than they could ever have learned otherwise.'

3. Ford's participation in motor racing '. . . is widely publicised proof of the performance we are capable of putting into the vehicles we build, and proof of the confidence we have in our ability to put it there. Nothing does more to sell a vehicle than respect and enthusiasm for it, and we believe that nothing generates enthusiasm for a car faster than winning in flat-out competition. Of course, the reverse side of the coin is that losing can hurt your product reputation, but that's a gamble we are willing to take.'

4. Our competition challenge in racing has made Ford a more competitive company, from the assembly lines to the executive suites. We all know we are in business to sell automobiles, not to win races – but that chequered flag is more dramatic, more stimulating and more exciting than a ten-day sales report.'

The Earliest Ford Competition Efforts

Despite their absence from the racing scene for very many years, the early years of this Century had seen Henry Ford build a number of interesting high-performance cars. Ford had built his first car in 1896 and in 1901 became the Superintendent of the Detroit Automobile Company, but that folded up later the same year after making only thirty horizontal-engined gas-buggies. In order to gain backing for his own car-production plans, Ford built a 26 hp 2-cylinder model with which he defeated a 40 hp Winton in the autumn of 1901.

The success of this first Ford Car encouraged him to build two more, 70 hp 4-cylinder beasts known as '999' and 'Arrow'. These were stark chassis, without proper body, clutch or gears. '999', distinguished by its two-handled steering tiller, was driven by Barney Oldfield in his first race in 1902, and once again defeated the Winton. A little later on, whether in 1903 or 1904 it is not certain, Henry Ford himself drove '999' over a mile of the frozen Lake St. Clair near New Baltimore, Michigan. This was a dramatic record attempt fully in the traditions of the birth of competitive motoring, for, to make a course, snow had to be cleared for four miles and cinders were then spread over the ice to provide wheelgrip. The vibration was atrocious and a mechanic had to ride on the bonnet to hold the throttle open. Ford's time for the mile was 39.4 seconds, a speed of 91·37 mph. This bettered Duray's kilometre record with a Gobron-Brillié by 6·64 mph, but was not recognised outside the United States.

Ford did not dabble further with competition cars, but in 1904 started car production under his own name. Whatever potential Henry Ford may have possessed as a builder of competition cars was never fully exploited, as his talents were devoted to mass-production cars and between the Autumn of 1908 and May, 1927 more than fifteen million Model-T Fords were made. Nevertheless, the Model-T appeared after the First World War on American race tracks, modified in various ways and almost invariably fitted with Chevrolet Frontenac heads. The most highly developed form of this cylinder head had 16 valves and twin overhead camshafts.

In the late 'thirties the use of a side-valve V-8 30 hp Ford engine became *de rigeur* in British trials and such cars as the Allard used Ford engines for trials, racing and road use. It was also the British Ford 1172 cc side-valve unit round which the 750 Motor Club based their exceptionally successful 1172 Formula. In 1963 Fords supplied special light alloy V-8 engines to power the Lotus cars which ran at Indianapolis, and it was in the same year and with basically the same power unit that Fords planned their own competition car.

The Concept of the Ford GT

The reasons why Ford should choose to enter sports car racing rather than the Grand Prix field are two-fold. Although the Grand

Prix car and the sports/racing prototype are both equally removed in concept from the normal touring car, there is little doubt that the ordinary motorist more closely associates an aerodynamically-enclosed sports car with his family saloon than he does an exposed-wheel single-seater. Secondly, although the Ford organisation is world-wide, Fords were primarily out to create an impression on the American public, and sports car racing is more familiar to them than Grand Prix events, which are not yet fully established on the American Continent.

The decision to take up racing was made in early 1963 and Fords were determined that the car should be raceworthy the following season – a proposal that gave Roy Lunn, who was in charge of the project, precious little time. Lunn was a young Englishman, and an early victim of the brain drain. He was born at Richmond in Surrey in 1925 and after being educated at Kingston Technical College and Leeds and Birmingham Universities, went to work for the AC Company at Thames Ditton in 1946. A year later he moved on to the Aston Martin organisation where, as assistant to Chief Designer Claude Hill, he was responsible for the mechanical design of the DB2, a car which won its class at Le Mans in 1950 and 1951. Barely two years had passed before Lunn again moved on, this time to the works of Jowett at Idle in Yorkshire. At Idle he was responsible for the development of the Jowett range of Javelin and Jupiter models, highly successful 1500 cc sporting cars with a flat-four engine and a general layout inspired by the Lancia Aprilia. Lunn evolved high-performance versions of the Jupiter sports 2-seater and these won their class at Le Mans in 1950, 1951 and 1952.

Unhappily, Jowetts ran into difficulties over the supply of bodies and production of all models ceased in late 1953. Lunn, who had been happy at Jowetts, was forced to move on again. He now took a job with the British Ford Company to start a vehicle Research Centre and the first project was the 105E Anglia. In 1956 Lunn became Car Product Planning Manager, but moved to the Dearborn Ford plant in 1958, where he worked in the Advanced Engineering Department. Here he was responsible for the concept of the 12M Taunus which was later put into production at the German Ford factory at Cologne. Promotion was speedy for a bright boy like Lunn, and he became Manager of the Vehicle Concepts Department in 1960.

In 1962 Lunn had been engaged on a project known as the Mustang

I sports car. Now this had absolutely no connection with the later production Mustang, but was an experimental show car. The same personnel that worked on this, which was powered by a mid-mounted Taunus engine driving the rear wheels (the production Taunus has front-wheel-drive), were set to work on the new sports/racing car project. Ford claim that the Mustang I served as a starting point for work, but in fact the only thing in common between the Mustang and the new project was the mid-engined layout. Since the acceptance of the rear-engined layout among racing car manufacturers, it had become the practice to achieve the best possible weight distribution by moving the engine ahead of the rear axle line, hence the expression 'mid-engined'. What Lunn and his staff were compelled to do was to look closely at existing rear-engined sports/racing cars such as the Ferraris and 'Bird-cage' Maseratis and base their design on these as far as they desired; but at the same time they took into account such features as likely increases in lap times and speeds along the Mulsanne Straight at Le Mans so that they could assess what demands would be made of the new design.

The enormous facilities and resources of the Ford Dearborn works were made full use of, and although Ford development costs were tremendously high by any standards, it should be remembered that they were primarily making use of resources that were already available and the vast expenditure was largely justified and necessitated by the urgency of the project. Ford engineers even used a computer which could work out handling characteristics in advance and save a great deal of track testing time absorbed in the more usual trial and error methods adopted by smaller constructors. Indeed, it was even possible, provided that the computer was fed the right programme, to use this to evolve body styles in accordance with the best aerodynamic principles.

Initial Ford studies were aimed at what they called 'package studies' and it was ascertained that all the essential components could be installed within a length of 156 inches, a height of 40 inches (from which the name GT40 was derived) and a wheelbase of 95 inches.

The 'package', as envisaged by Lunn, consisted of a coupé body with a forward-hinged canopy top, fixed seats and movable controls with, behind the seats, twin radiators with side ducting, fuel tanks along the sides, oil tank, battery and forward mounted spare wheel. The power unit was to be the Indianapolis 4·2-litre unit, and this is discussed later. Ford had available no suitable form of transmission and it was decided to use the Italian-made Colotti combined rear axle and final drive unit, known in American terminology as a 'transaxle'.

In the meantime, a full-size clay model of the proposed car had been built. Its shape was largely a matter of guesswork, as it was anticipated that the GT40 would be capable of speeds in excess of 200 mph and there was precious little knowledge available of road forms for that speed. From this model two steps forward were made. It was found that the side-ducting of the radiator gave negligible heat dissipation and it was decided to adopt two separate doors, as it was not clear whether the hinged canopy would satisfy the requirements of the Federation Internationale de l'Automobile.

The summer of 1963 saw Ford make a drastic policy change by calling in an outside expert. The reasons are logical enough and the choice could not have been wiser, for the man chosen, Eric Broadley, had already built cars that conformed very closely to the Ford project. In publicity about the GT40, little mention is made of Broadley, but it was clear why he had been brought in on the project. Ford's ambition was to have cars raceworthy for the 1964 season, and time was running out. To get a car racing within fourteen months of starting from scratch is virtually impossible and it probably could never have been done without Broadley. Numerous problems that would face Ford had already faced Broadley, and he had already found many of the answers. Nevertheless, one cannot help feeling that Ford would prefer to forget about the designer from Bromley who made their plans possible. Equally, Broadley was not entirely happy within the Ford Organisation. He had been used to working as his own master and relying on his own, admittedly limited, resources. With Ford, he became a small, if very well paid, cog in a vast machine. As Broadley was the key man behind the GT 40 project, it is worth paying close attention to his earlier achievements.

The Lola Story

The earliest Lolas were specials built by Eric and Graham Broadley at Bromley in Kent and the first car made its appearance in 1956. When Eric took up car design on a full-time basis and gave up his former occupation as a builder, elder brother Graham continued to run the family tailor's shop in Bromley. The first Lola to make a serious impression on the racing scene was an 1100 cc Coventry-Climax powered car that proved more than a match for the contemporary Lotus. However, in the early days the Lola Équipe was not always as well organised as was desirable and in the 1958 Tourist Trophy at Goodwood, nine valuable minutes were lost because the team had no suitable spare wheel – it was necessary to repair a puncture in the pits.

For 1960 Broadley built a very pretty front-engined Formula Junior single-seater, followed by a rear-engined design for the same Formula, but it was not long before he had graduated to greater things. The Bowmaker-Yeoman team, successor to the Yeoman Credit team which had raced Coopers during the years 1960–61, contracted him to build a team of Grand Prix cars for the 1962 season. The team manager was Reg Parnell, who had formerly been in charge of the Aston Martin team and was a very successful ex-racing driver, and he was assisted by former Aston Martin mechanics. The team drivers were John Surtees and Roy Salvadori. The Lola Grand Prix car had the familiar layout of a V-8 Coventry-Climax engine mounted at the rear, but it was one of the smallest and lightest cars of the Formula and was only just above the minimum weight limit. Although the Lola won no Grandes Épreuves (events counting towards the World Championship), which was hardly to be expected of a new car, the performance was very satisfactory, especially in the hands of John Surtees. Unfortunately, Bowmaker-Yeoman decided to withdraw from racing after running in the Tasman Formula events held during the winter of 1962–3. Surtees joined the Ferrari team and Broadley became involved in another equally exciting project.

When the new car made its debut at the 1963 Racing Car Show at Olympia, it was the sensation of the show, despite its arriving late after a tremendous rush to get it there and with certain vital parts missing. The new car was known simply as the Lola GT, it was built to comply with the FIA's regulations for Grand Touring Prototypes and it was, at the same time, breathtakingly beautiful and overtly fierce. In broad outline it consisted of an aerodynamic fixed-head coupé powered by a production Ford V-8 4·2-litre engine, tuned with Shelby modifications to develop 260 bhp at 6500 rpm and mounted at the rear. The engine modifications included four twin-choke downdraught Weber carburettors. Transmission was by a Colotti 4-speed gearbox in unit with the final drive. It is interesting to note that a similar form of transmission was used on the Lotus Indianapolis cars.

In detail, there was a monocoque central chassis section forming a stiff, but light, wide and uncluttered passenger compartment. The basis of the central section was a pair of large box-members which formed the door sills on either side and also served as fuel tanks. The inner face of each box-member was made from sheet steel bent to a U-section, whereas the outer part was duralumin sheet. Inside were four cast magnesium formers with bosses to take the attachment bolts for the door frame and roof structure. Between the two side-members was a steel floor pan with small boxed bracing members on which the seats and the housing for the central remote control gearchange were mounted.

At the rear of each side-member there was a fabricated extension terminating in a built-up 'pyramid box' to which the combined coil-spring and damper units were attached. Running between the two pyramid boxes was a tubular ladder-type member which could be detached to facilitate engine removal. Tubular members ran back from the pyramids to carry the body-supporting pivots. The rear suspension itself consisted of symmetrical A-shaped wishbones at the lower ends of the cast magnesium hub-carriers and at the upper ends these were transverse links and long forward-facing radius arms that ran to pivot points above the ends of a triangular cross-member. This was a particularly satisfactory suspension arrangement, as it gave excellent control of wheel movement especially under driving and braking torque.

From the scuttle forwards there was a mainly square-section tubular structure extending to provide the front suspension mountings and to carry the cross-flow radiators and the spare wheel. Front suspension was by unequal length wishbones. Saab rack-and-pinion steering was used and, indeed, the car possessed quite a large number of minor proprietary fittings, including Ford Cortina rear lights and Triumph Herald fastening catches used for securing the front and rear body panels which hinged at each end of the car. As the Lola GT weighed only 16 cwt, it had the excellent power-to-weight ratio of 325 bhp per ton.

The Lola GT made its racing debut in the *Daily Express* International Trophy meeting at Silverstone in May, 1963. It had been intended that John Surtees should drive the car, but he was under contract to Ferrari and the Ferrari team manager withdrew his

Above: The first of the rear-engined Ferraris was the Tipo 246/SP, which had a V-6 2417 c.c. engine developing 270 b.h.p. and ran at Le Mans in 1961. This car, shared by Richie Ginther and Wolfgang von Trips, was eliminated by running out of fuel. The race was won by a front-engined V-12 'Testa Rossa' Ferrari. *Below:* The Lola on its last race appearance at Brands Hatch in 1963. The general similarity in concep to the Ford GT40 can easily be seen

Above: A Shelby American Daytona Coupé at speed in the 1965 Daytona 2000 kms. race. A Daytona shared by Keck, Johnson and Schlesser took second place overall. *Below:* Race debut for the Ford G.T. was in the 1964 Nürburgring 1000 kilometres race, where the single car entered made second fastest time in practice, but retired after $2\frac{1}{2}$ hours racing with failure of a suspension bracket

consent at the last moment, so works Cooper driver Tony Maggs took his place. As he had never driven the car previously and did not even have the chance to practice – and it was undoubtedly a formidable piece of machinery for a driver not accustomed to such power – Maggs did well to take ninth place overall and finish on the same lap as the winner. An entry was next made in the Nurburgring 1000 kilometres race where it was driven by Maggs and Bob Olthoff, and it was the *only* entry in its class. After starting well, it was delayed by a rear wheel working loose and damaging the driving pins. A lengthy pit stop was spent sorting out this trouble and the car then continued to run well until eliminated by a distributor drive failure.

Broadley had managed to secure an entry at Le Mans, and here his drivers were Dick Attwood and David Hobbs (the latter usually seen at the wheel of an automatic transmission Lotus Elite), provided with a brand new car. Delay with a slipping dynamo belt caused the Lola to fall back, but by 10 pm it had risen to 15th place and 12th by midnight. Further delays were caused by a broken selector-arm bolt in the gearbox and the eventual result was seen just before six on the Sunday morning, when Hobbs found himself unable to engage third gear as he rushed down from Dunlop Bridge to the Esses. The car bounced from bank to bank and was wrecked. The Lola made one further appearance, the August Bank Holiday Brands Hatch meeting, where it retired with falling oil pressure after only two laps.

The Blending of Ideas

It was at this time that Broadley accepted Ford's offer. In August also, Ford held out the bait to John Wyer to join the project and he accepted. Wyer was probably the most experienced team manager in the country, in which role he had acted for Aston Martin for several years before becoming their technical director. He had learnt nearly all there was to know about running a sports car team through trial and error. At Aston Martins he had made mistakes and learnt from them. He knew when he knew the answer to a problem and when he did not; and when he knew it, he made sure that everyone else knew it as well. Ford had purchased two of the Lola prototypes and started an elaborate testing and evaluation programme with one car at the British Goodwood circuit and with one car at the Ford Dearborn works. This had been completed by the end of

August, 1963. New premises were acquired at Slough and the set-up was given the title of Ford Advanced Vehicles Limited, the Company being a subsidiary of the English Ford organisation, and managed by John Wyer. Broadley's original contract was for a twelve-month period, but it was subsequently extended by six months.

Much of the early testing of the cars was done by Bruce McLaren, the Cooper works driver who had been introduced to European racing by Jack Brabham. McLaren remained with Coopers until the end of the 1965 season. Then, like Brabham, having learnt all he could from Coopers, he went off to build competition cars on his own. His experiences with the Ford project have assisted him to a considerable extent in the development of his own sports/racing cars. From Ford's point of view he represented the ideal test driver. He has a cheerful disposition, he does not expect the car to be automatically *au point* and set up to his own tastes, and he has the patience to wait while mechanics sort out any problems.

It was at this stage, when under Roy Lunn's control the amalgamation of Lunn's own ideas and the best features of the Lola started, that the story becomes confusing, and it is almost impossible to analyse in detail which is which. In September, 1963, the centre of activity was shifted from Dearborn to Slough, and to the Buckinghamshire works there was transferred the group of Ford engineers working on the project together with car layouts, models and existing components. Lunn had broken the design and development of the car down into seven convenient compartments:

>Aerodynamics
>Engine
>Transmission
>Body
>Suspension, steering, brakes, wheels
>Interior layout
>Fuel system

Aerodynamics

After the completion of the initial 'package' and shape studies, a $\frac{3}{8}$-scale aerodynamic model had been constructed and a series of tests carried out in the wind tunnel at the University of Maryland. Early in the tests it became clear that although the proposed body shape was satisfactory from the point of view of drag, the tendency to lift at over 200 mph amounted to over half the weight of the car. By adopting a low nose shape, the tendency to lift was reduced, but it was only completely eliminated when 'spoilers' were added under the front end; the Ford engineers were astonished to discover that the addition of these also had the effect of reducing the drag.

The calculations made at this time indicated that the car would be capable of 215 mph, but it emerged subsequently that 76 of the available 350 bhp was absorbed in internal ducting such as radiators, brake ducts, engine air and interior ventilation. Only 30 bhp had been allowed for these items in the original calculations, and the original GT40s were capable of only (!) 197 mph in still air.

The Engine

With the availability of the special Indianapolis Ford engines, these were obviously used in place of the tuned production engine by which the Lola had been powered. The Indianapolis engine was a development of the production 'Fairlane' unit, but had been very extensively re-worked. This was a pushrod overhead valve engine with a five main bearing crankshaft and chosen in preference to the twin overhead camshaft unit which was used in later Indianapolis events. Unlike the production Fairlane engine, this had a special aluminium cylinder block and heads and dry sump lubrication. In its Indianapolis form, 370 bhp was developed at 7000 rpm, but detuned to run on pump fuel (instead of the exotic blends permitted at the 'brickyard') and with the addition of an alternator and starter motor, this became 350 bhp at 7200 rpm – an increase of 90 bhp over the output of Broadley's original Lola. Compression ratio was 12·5 : 1, four twin-choke Weber carburettors were used and there was a tuned 'cross-over' exhaust system.

Transmission

This was another major design feature which both Broadley's Lola and Lunn's original concept had in common. When Broadley designed the Lola he was forced, like most other small constructors, to use a proprietary gearbox and final drive unit, for this is too expensive and elaborate a unit to tackle with limited resources. Lunn favoured a proprietory unit mainly because of the time factor. British proprietary transmission units were not sufficiently advanced but in Italy Valeiro Colotti, a former Maserati technician, had set up in business on his own and specialised in transmission units. Despite having only four ratios and non-syncromesh engagement of the gears, the Colotti was felt to be the only unit at the time that would be capable of handling the power output of the Ford with reliability. This was mounted in the chassis immediately behind the 8½-inch twin-plate clutch.

From the gearbox the drive was taken to the rear wheels by drive shafts with single Cardan universal joints at the outboard end and pot joints inboard. However, rubber couplings were later selected for the inboard end in an attempt to smooth out harshness and generally improve the reliability of the transmission line.

The Body and Chassis

In general design of the body and chassis Lunn and Broadley were thinking along the same lines before they collaborated, although this does not mean to say that Lunn's original conception of the car was not in any way inspired by what he had already seen of the Lola. As on the Lola, the load-bearing basis of the monocoque chassis was a unitised underbody with box-side sills forming the fuel tanks. This was constructed from thin sheet steel, as Lunn felt that the use of special lightweight alloys would consume valuable development time. The chassis was completed by two main bulkheads, a roof section and structures front and rear to carry suspension mountings.

The latter were of a less complex nature than those fitted to the Lola. Front and rear sub-frames were added to provide for the body supports, for the mounting of the spare wheel, the radiator and the battery mounting, and to provide supports for the quick-lift jacks.

Although externally the 'package' generally resembled the Lola and the overall dimensions were similar, the Ford GT had a new and very pugnacious body style. The doors were cut extensively into the roof to provide easy entry and exit (a boon for Le Mans starts!) and these together with the bonnet and boot panels and the rocker panels were made of hand-laminated fibreglass. Very great care was taken to ensure that the air-flow was not disturbed by projections and all the body fittings were flush with the body panels. The windscreen and other glass on the body were attached by special adhesives. Construction of the bodies was carried out by Abbey Panels, a Coventry concern of vast experience which had also been responsible for building the bodies of both the Jaguar C-type and the Aston Martin DB3S.

Suspension, Steering, Brakes and Wheels

Design of the suspension was restricted by a number of factors: the size of the car imposed space limitations; the very low weight of the basic structure meant that it was necessary to spread the suspension attachments points to reduce the loading and strain at every point; the suspension units had to be adjustable so that the car could be set up to suit different circuits; high-speed aerodynamic tests had revealed the need for what Roy Lunn describes as 'anti' features; and above all the resulting compromise had to provide excellent roadholding characteristics.

The front suspension followed Broadley's practice, with double tubular bronze-welded wishbones with the axes of the inner pivots inclined horizontally at 30 degrees to the centre line of the car to reduce front end dive under hard braking. At the rear the suspension again followed the Lola, with A-shaped wishbones, trailing links running from the main rear bulkhead and transverse links. The angling of the wishbones to the cast magnesium suspension uprights coupled with the linkage geometry was arranged specifically to prevent rear-end lift at speed. This was one feature of the design which involved extensive use of the computer. After the basic suspension linkage layout had been settled, a programme was formulated which took into account all the factors involved in the many links of the suspension moving in different planes and on canted axes. From the results obtained, curves could be plotted to meet a given condition – this process considerably speeded up the design process and aided reaching a decision about the compromises involved. This was probably the first time that a computer was used in the design of a competition car.

Rack-and-pinion steering was chosen. This had a ratio of 16 : 1 and required $2\frac{1}{4}$ turns of the steering wheel from lock to lock. For braking, solid cast-iron discs, $11\frac{1}{2}$ inches in diameter and $\frac{1}{2}$-inch thick, were used with Girling racing calipers – again as on the Lola. The braking system incorporated separate master cylinders front and rear and these had a balance mechanism for adjusting brake distribution. It had originally been planned to use cast magnesium wheels, as on the Lola, but there were development snags, so the earliest cars had Italian Borrani wire wheels (15-inch) with 6½-inch alloy rims at the front and 8-inch at the rear.

The Interior Layout

As the cars were intended exclusively for long-distance racing, driver comfort was regarded as a very important consideration. Following the layout used on the Mustang I, the GT40 was fitted with a fixed driving seat and pedals mounted on a cast alloy adjustable member. This arrangement offered structural advantages and provided snug support round the driver to help prevent fatigue from high-speed cornering effects. The basic support medium of the driving seat was a nylon netting covered with a ventilated pad to help evaporate driver perspiration. Great care was also taken to ensure that the faces of the instruments pointed directly at the driver so as to minimise distortion and reflection. Flow-through ventilation was provided, together with full protection from adverse weather conditions. Ducts, running from the nose of the car through the body sides and doors into the engine compartment, provided an airflow on to the fuel pumps and exhaust pipes. For the carburettors, air was drawn from ducts in the side of the roof.

The Fuel System

The two side fuel tanks held a total of 42 US gallons. Each had its own filler cap, fuel pick-up box and individual electric pumps feeding a common supply pipe to the carburettors. One of the tanks also had a reserve pick-up unit. Inside the steel tanks there was inserted neoprene bags for safety reasons in the event of a crash and a plate supported from the top inspection cover acted as a baffle. As previously mentioned, the prime advantage of these side fuel tanks was that the handling was not affected by a fall in fuel level during the race.

The testing of components and the main design work had been completed by the end of November, 1963 and during that winter the Ford engineers devoted themselves to settling details of the design, getting together the required components and building the first two prototypes. Eleven months after the initial design studies had started at Dearborn, the first GT40 was completed on 1st April, 1964. Ten days later the second car was completed. There was now a frantic rush to get the cars ready in time for Le Mans practice session on 18th/19th April. Bad weather conditions prevented extensive testing at Goodwood, as had been intended, and further time had been wasted by flying the first of the cars to New York for Ford executives to see and flying it back again for Le Mans.

At Le Mans the cars were far from right, lacking speed and needing a great deal of detail adjustment. The practice day was very wet and Frenchman Jo Schlesser, driving the first car to be built, got into a tremendous slide caused by aquaplaning at the corner at the end of the Mulsanne straight and spun off. The car was severely damaged but Schlesser was unhurt. The second car was also damaged in a collision, but less seriously.

A lot of hard work and development was still needed before the cars could be regarded as raceworthy.

SIX
1964

Ferrari Developments

At the beginning of the 1964 season Enzo Ferrari was not especially concerned with the possible threat from Fords. It was rather a case of Ford setting their sights on victory at Le Mans, in 1964 if possible, and that meant defeating Ferrari. Ferrari was more concerned with the Grand Prix field and waging his prolonged battle with BRM and Lotus. Sports car development, however, did continue at Maranello and the 1963 Paris Salon saw the appearance of an exciting new car. This was the 250LM, intended as a competitor in the Grand Touring category, but directly evolved from the 1963 250/P 3-litre sports/racing car. Mechanical differences were slight and the primary difference was the closed bodywork of the 250LM.

It was over this car that Enzo Ferrari had a serious row with the Federation Internationale de l'Automobile, did not stop screaming about the situation all summer and eventually fell out with his National Club as well. For a car to be homologated in the Grand Touring category by the FIA it was, strictly speaking, necessary for one hundred of the model to have been built. These rules have always been interpreted by the FIA with flexibility. Thus, the FIA did not object to such cars as the lightweight competition Jaguar E-type, which was a direct development of the production E-type, but had fuel injection, a 5-speed gearbox, an alloy body and a large number of alloy castings that were non-standard; nor did they object to the GTO Ferrari, of which less than 40 were built, because it was a direct development of the original Ferrari 250GT. The 250LM, however, had nothing in common with any previous GT Ferrari, and when it was put forward for homologation production did not amount to double figures. Apart from this, the homologation committee of the FIA objected to the attempt to mislead them, for

WINNING FERRARIS *Above:* The rear-engined 3-litre V-12 Tipo 250/P of John Surtees and Willy Mairesse which took first place in the 1963 Nürburgring 1000 kilometres race. *Below:* At Le Mans in 1964 victory went to the 3·3-litre Tipo 275/P Ferrari of Guichet/Vaccarella entered by the works

Following the encouraging performance of the Ford at the Nürburgring three ran at Le Mans the following month. All three retired. This is the car driven by Phil Hill and Bruce McLaren which was eliminated by gearbox trouble. The second car is the Aston Martin of Sutcliffe and Salmon

they had been induced to believe that nearly 100 cars had been built. After a little while Ferrari again presented the 250LM for homologation, when some 14 had been completed, and again it was refused. By now the 250LM had the 3·3-litre engine and in accordance with normal Ferrari designations should have been known as the 275LM (the number represented the capacity of one cylinder). To perpetuate the myth that the cars were being produced in fair numbers Ferrari continued to use the old designation.

Two things annoyed Ferrari about this situation. Firstly, he felt that he was being singled out for unfair treatment and that other constructors had been allowed to have models homologated of which only very few had been produced, e.g. the AC Daytona coupé. He did appear to overlook, however, that the AC had at least a chassis layout in common with a production model. Secondly, until the car was homologated, he had great difficulty in persuading customers to buy it. He had been hoping to sell some thirty or forty cars to private owners who would mop up the Cobras in the GT category, while he was concentrating on the prototypes. Furthermore, he was expecting the Italian Automobile Club to fix the situation with the FIA so that the car would be homologated. But a bar to the Italian Automobile Club fixing anything was that the German Porsche Company *had* built 100 of their radically new 904 Grand Touring model before homologation. At this point Enzo Ferrari turned nasty and uttered threats of giving up racing or, at least, not racing in Italy. As if to prove that this time he really meant it, he surrendered his racing licence towards the end of the 1964 season and his Formula One cars appeared in the United States and Mexican Grands Prix in American blue and white racing colours and in the name of the North American Racing Team. By the beginning of the 1965 season, however, Ferrari had forgotten about the dispute and went on racing as usual.

In the prototype category Ferrari raced two models, both of which were basically the same as the cars raced in 1963 and featuring similar tubular frames, fully independent suspension, 5-speed gearboxes and the engine mounted behind the cockpit and ahead of the rear axle. The first of these, the 275/P, was identical to the previous year's 250/P apart from having the larger 3286 cc (77 × 58·8 mm) engine and developing 320 bhp at 7700 rpm on a 9·8 : 1 compression ratio. The other was the 330/P which had a 3967 cc (77 × 71 mm) engine with a power output of 370 bhp at 7200 rpm on a compression ratio of 8·8 : 1. These cars made a successful debut in the Sebring 12-hours race, where they faced nothing in the way of serious opposition. After the 330/P shared by John Surtees and Lorenzo Bandini lost the lead through a long pit stop with electrical trouble, the smaller car of Mike Parkes and Umberto Maglioli had won from a similar car of Scarfiotti and Vaccarella.

One of the strengths of the Ferrari organisation was its excellent team of drivers. This team was, however, split by a certain amount of dissension between British and Italian members. John Surtees is one of the most devoted and enthusiastic drivers in racing and by 1964 he had rid himself of the rather wild enthusiasm that had marred his early days in motor, as opposed to motor-cycle, racing. He would always go to great pains to see that he was fit for a race and would ensure that his car was equally fit by taking the time and trouble to explain in detail what was wrong with it to the mechanical staff. In this he was well backed up by Mike Parkes, the son of the Chairman of the British Alvis Company, who combined the talents of racing driver, test driver and development engineer. Parkes was regarded as a steady and reliable driver with the right temperament for long-distance sports car racing. At 33 he was cool enough not to overdo it through an excess of enthusiasm, and his mechanical knowledge gave him a decided edge over other drivers in diagnosing peculiar noises made by a car and nursing a sick one to the finish.

The weak link in the team was Eugenio Dragoni, the team manager, who knew little about either motor racing or men, and who in little ways put the backs up both of Surtees and Parkes. An example of this was quoted in the last chapter – his refusal to permit Surtees to drive the Lola at Silverstone in 1963. Furthermore, as an Italian he favoured the leading Italian in the team, Lorenzo Bandini, who tended to be given preferential treatment. Bandini's career with Ferrari had been somewhat chequered, as he had first joined the team in 1962, while the following season he returned to the Scuderia Centro-Sud who had previously used his services. This was because Ferrari felt that his drivers should be employed on a full-time basis and always be available for testing work. Bandini, however, had business interests which occupied part of his time, but he had rejoined Ferrari for 1964. One of Ferrari's reasons for relenting on this point was the importance he placed on having an Italian in his team.

In April was the Targa Florio, an event first held in 1906, and

58 years later the Sicilian roads maintained for this race a second-to-none reputation as a car-breaker. Although this race counted towards the Manufacturers' Championship, Ferrari did not enter, preferring to concentrate for the time being on sorting out his Grand Prix cars and conserving his energies for the Nurbürgring 1000 kilometres race and Le Mans. Apart from these considerations, the Targa Florio was the race in which Ferrari stood the least chance of winning, for it favoured the smaller cars. Victory went, in fact, to one of the 904GTS Porsche entries recently homologated by the FIA as a Grand Touring car.

Ford Developments

After the débâcle of the Le Mans test weekend, Broadley and the Ford team went back to Slough to sort out their problems. The most serious problem was that there was a noticeable instability at high speeds, an instability that had not revealed itself during the wind tunnel tests. Within one week of returning to England the problem had been solved during testing at the Motor Industry Research Association proving ground. This was what Roy Lunn had described as an aerostability condition which caused a rotary motion of the rear end of the vehicle comparable to that of an arrow without feathers. This motion increased with speed, and at Le Mans had been accentuated by the wet surface until the point at which the rear end had lost adhesion. A 'duck-tail' spoiler was added to the Fords and this not only had the effect of putting 'feathers on the arrow', but slightly reduced drag; the spoiler moved the centre of air pressure further to the rear and helped force the tail of the car down on to the road. The effect of the spoiler was felt at as low a speed as 70 mph. One of the most interesting aspects of this problem is that other constructors whose bodies were less scientifically designed have not had this trouble. The story goes that Colin Chapman once asked a Ferrari technician why the Maranello cars had spoilers. Back came the answer: 'to prevent fuel spilling on the hot exhaust during refuelling'.

The Nurbürgring 1000 Kilometres Race

This event held in May marked the debut for the Ford GT, and the second car built, repaired after its Le Mans shunt, was entered for Phil Hill and Bruce McLaren. Certainly John Wyer did not anticipate the Ford winning, but it was essential that a car should be tried out under proper racing conditions before Le Mans.

There were only two works Ferraris, a 275/P driven by Surtees and Bandini and another one for Scarfiotti and Vaccarella, but a similar car had been loaned to Maranello Concessionaires. This was driven by Graham Hill and Innes Ireland, but with *his* record at the Nurbürgring nobody expected Ireland to remain in the race for long. These three cars were the stars of the race, but among the supporting cast were the private 275LMs of the Équipe Nationale Belge driven by 'Beurlys' and Pierre Dumay and Maglioli/Jochen Rindt. Porsche often do unexpectedly well, and were strong outsiders, especially as they were on home territory, and everyone was keeping a wary eye on the works 904 coupés. Two of these were prototypes with 2-litre flat-8-cylinder engines derived from the unit that Porsche used in Grand Prix racing. Apart from the works Cobras, there was an exciting entry that included privately-owned GTO Ferraris, lightweight E-type Jaguars, a special Lister-Jaguar that had run at Le Mans in 1963 and also an Iso Grifo.

As there were 81 starters, the first lap of the 22·81-kilometre course was a high-speed traffic jam, and was enlivened by a Cobra being smashed up the rear by a German-entered Jaguar and a Lancia Flavia coupé spinning so that a 904 Porsche could not help hitting it broadside. Each time an incident like this occurred, the rest of the field following had to make an emergency stop. One result of this was that, at the end of the first lap the GTO Ferrari of Lucien Bianchi, one of the fastest drivers in sports cars racing, which finished fourth, was lying 56th! At this stage the blue and white Ford with Phil Hill at the wheel was second behind Surtees' Ferrari, but the other two 275/Ps were snapping at Hill's heels. One by one they squeezed past, as Hill was slowed with gear selector trouble but his was the only car that managed to stay in the mirrors of the pack of howling Ferraris. After 11 laps the Ford came in for refuelling and McLaren took over. Four laps later the Ford became overdue, but eventually crept round into the pits, and after a brief inspection was withdrawn.

The Ferraris were now completely unchallenged, but Vaccarella had taken the lead from Bandini and Ireland was closing up. Dragoni began to flap and asked Ronnie Hoare if he would slow the Maranello car down so as to prevent the Ferraris from dicing each other into the ground. Amused by the situation, Hoare suggested that Dragoni should slow the works cars down. At the end of 28 laps Vaccarella held a slender lead over Ireland and Surtees had taken over from Bandini, but was in third place after a frantic and unnecessarily early stop for fuel by the Italian. A lap later, and only just before the car had reached the pits Ireland ran out of petrol. The regulations did not permit the car to be refuelled away from the pits. However, an official assured Hoare that it would be in order for a can to be taken out to the car and Hill ran off with one. When the car reached the pits it was refuelled and re-joined the race, only to be black-flagged because the official had been wrong. It was subsequently found that the Ferrari had a split fuel tank, so all the effort was wasted anyway. A mere three laps later disaster struck again in the Ferrari camp, when Surtees' car had the right-hand rear axle-shaft break, shedding the wheel and hub into the bushes, where the car soon followed. Surtees was unhurt, and to reduce the risk of anything happening to the remaining 275/P it was slowed right off, and finished a lap ahead of a GTO in second place.

The reason for the withdrawal of the Ford was the failure of a rear suspension mounting bracket because of an incorrect welding process. When the vehicle was examined at Slough, however, it became obvious that a number of other welding points were near failure. The team had learnt an important lesson from the Nurbürgring, and improvements were incorporated in the three cars being built for the Le Mans race.

Le Mans

The fascination of Le Mans for the British is probably not matched by another happening on the Continent. Each June sees an exodus through the Channel ports and Lydd airfield of motor-racing enthusiasts crammed with sleeping bags, primus stoves, Kodak Instamatics and the current copy of *Motor Sport* into cars of every description, from side-valve Ford Populars (surely the *lowest* form of motoring life) to the DB6 and Iso Rivolta of the affluent. N.138 to Le Mans becomes a race track itself, with overheating and over-laden Minis trying to out-corner Cobras and the owners of the TRs intent on proving that they can out-drag any MGB – and God help the poor Citroën or Renault driver who happens to be going the other way. The police become resigned to leaving the roads to the English and content themselves with trying to cope with the traffic jams around the circuit itself. The French police, incidentally, can *really* cope with traffic jams, not just complicate them, as do their English counterparts.

For some the racing is the least of the fascinations at the track. The French retain that peculiarly perverted humour which revels in such sights as the leopard woman from Borneo and the fat, bearded lady, both regulars of the sideshows in the cheaper public enclosure. And where else, even in France, do you have to pay the equivalent of 3/- for a bottle of coke? Over the years there occur more deaths, whether by design or chance, in the spectators' enclosures than have ever been caused by the cars – including the 1955 disaster. Undoubtedly, however, the presence of the mighty Ford organisation brought tremendous added interest to the 1964 race.

Ford's three cars were driven by Phil Hill and Bruce McLaren, Richie Ginther and Masten Gregory, Jo Schlesser and Richard Attwood. Le Mans was a circuit which appealed to Hill, and he had already won there three times previously with Ferraris. He certainly had no apprehensions about the race, while McLaren knew the Ford better than anybody. Of the other drivers, Ginther was another vastly experienced American, also a former Ferrari team member and in 1964 number 2 in the Formula One BRM team. Gregory could be described as a good second-classer with bags of sports car experience with Jaguars, Listers, Maseratis and Cobras. Schlesser was another experienced sports car driver, but there was doubt that he had rather lost confidence in the Ford after his practice week-end crash. Attwood was comparatively inexperienced at Le Mans, but he was reserve driver for BRM. The McLaren/Hill car was the first to be built and was 50lb. heavier than the others. At scrutineering the fuel tanks of the Fords were found to hold more than the 140-litre maximum permitted and the excess capacity was taken up with displacement blocks.

Facing the Fords were eight prototype Ferraris:

330/P: John Surtees/Lorenzo Bandini
275/P: Jean Guichet/Nino Vaccarella
275/P: Mike Parkes/Lodovico Scarfiotti
275/P: Giancarlo Baghetti/Umberto Maglioli
330/P: Graham Hill/Joakim Bonnier (a loan to Maranello Concessionaires)
330/P: Pedro Rodriguez/Skip Hudson (on loan to North American Racing Team)

275LM: Pierre Dumay/Langlois van Ophem (entered by Équipe Nationale Belge)
275LM: David Piper/Jochen Rindt (entered by North American Racing Team)

A formidable array, and there was no doubt that any one of these eight cars was a potential winner. Since the Nurbürgring 1000 kilometres race, when Ireland had dropped out on the circuit with a leaking fuel tank, the sill tanks running the whole length of the Ferraris between the wheels had been reconstructed using light alloy, with re-arranged baffles and local glass-fibre reinforcement. At scrutineering it was noticed that the screwed spring collars of the Koni dampers which controlled the height of the cars were at their top limit, and Dragoni was given a strict warning that they were not to be lowered. Another formidable entry, but in view of Maserati's record at Le Mans, not expected to last long, was a vast V-8 5-litre Maserati entered by Maserati France, the concessionaires, as Maserati themselves no longer raced, and driven by the veteran Maurice Trintignant and André Simon. This Maserati was a development of the Tipo 151 cars that Briggs Cunningham and Maserati France had run at Le Mans in 1962. It now featured a version of the V-8 four overhead camshaft Maserati engine of 4911 cc (94×89 mm) and with Lucas fuel injection. A Maserati 5-speed gearbox was in unit with the final drive. The chassis was a multi-tubular structure on the space-frame principle with wishbone and coil spring front suspension and a de Dion rear axle. Fierce looking fixed-head coupé bodywork was fitted, and in many ways the car was reminiscent of the Ferraris at Le Mans ten years previously. The overwhelming swing to the rear-engined layout was seen in that cars with this layout outnumbered those with the power unit in front of the driver by 31 to 28

Although there were scheduled 55 starters and four cars non-started, and there was certain to be a strong dice in the Grand Touring category between the GTO Ferraris, the Cobras and the Aston Martin of Mike Salmon and Peter Sutcliffe, there were no other contenders for outright victory unless all the faster cars fell by the wayside – in which case victory would go conceivably to one of the works Porsche entries.

The minutes leading up to four pm on the Saturday of the Le Mans race are probably the most nerve-racking time in the motor racing year. While the crowds are still pouring into the circuit, while the spectators in the enclosures in the terrace opposite the pits are desperately straining their necks to see the cars (and only those on the upper tiers can see them), the anxious drivers stand in a long line opposite their cars waiting for the fall of the flag. This is the moment of panic, a panic that affects almost all drivers, for there are few whose *sang froid* is sufficient for them to be unaffected by thoughts of what can go wrong during the ensuing 24 hours, from fears that the button will fail to start the engine and the possibility of being eliminated right at the start in a traffic jam prang, to speculations as to the mechanical reliability of the cars, crashes in the night and the hundred and one troubles that beset them in practice.

Right at the start of the race the three Ferraris of Surtees, Hill and Rodriguez shot into the lead with Ginther's Ford in hot pursuit, but the Ford, unkindly described by some journalists as a Lola-Ford, had soon slipped past the Maranello cars and began to build up an enormous lead. The car shared by Attwood and Schlesser was well placed in the first ten and could be speeded up if the leader ran into mechanical trouble. All was not well, however, with the third of the Anglo-American cars, as Hill only managed to get away from the start over a minute behind the other cars, and it popped and banged its way round the circuit, twice coming into the pits to try and cure the trouble. This eventually traced to a blocked carburettor jet, and once this had been cured Hill started to make up lost ground. At the end of the first hour he was lying 44th, but by the end of the 13th hour had moved up to fourth position. When the leading Ford came in to refuel, the pit staff made a terrible mess of the job and the lead was lost to Surtees' Ferrari. Disaster struck the Ford team in the fifth hour. While travelling at full speed along the Mulsanne Straight the Attwood/Schlesser car caught fire as the result of a broken fuel line. The driver was unhurt, but the car was partially burnt out. At the second fuel stop Ginther handed over to Gregory, but the Ford was soon back in the pits with gearbox trouble. After a long stop, during which the Ford mechanics made a futile attempt to cure the trouble, the car was withdrawn.

The remaining Ford, however, was going faster and faster, and by the early hours of Sunday morning it had climbed to third place ahead of the Surtees 330/P which had lost a lot of time repairing a broken petrol pipe and had then been delayed by an internal leak which had caused overheating and a loss of water. Another Ferrari in trouble was the Maranello Concessionaires car of Bonnier and

Hill, which was also losing water and had stopped to change a collapsed rear wheel. The remaining blue and white car was, however, flattering only to deceive, for after setting a new absolute lap record of 3 min 49·4 sec, it too came into the pits with gearbox trouble. Ford felt that they could patch the car up sufficiently to get it running, but it was withdrawn, because they did not want to see it lagging along at the back of the field. The fastest Ford along the Mulsanne Straight was the McLaren/Hill car, which had been timed at 187·5 mph, comparing not unfavourably with the fastest car, the Maserati, at 191·3 mph. The Maserati, incidentally, retired with electrical failure. After 4½ hours racing this car had held third place.

Although they were not without troubles of their own, there were sufficient prototype Ferraris still running to dominate the overall picture. The NART entry of Rodriguez and Hudson retired after only 4¼ hours with a burst oil radiator. In the first hour Parkes and Scarfiotti were delayed by a stop to replace the distributor, and after seven hours racing this promising entry went out with a suspected broken piston. The Baghetti and Maglioli car was eliminated by a collision with a Cobra at White House, and this accident cost the lives of three spectators who had wandered to the side of the track from the spectator enclosure. In general the transmissions of the prototype Ferraris were not able to match the increased power output and all except the winner suffered from clutch slip at some time during the race. In the latter stages more than one was suffering from a loss of compression, and although this did not affect their running, there were anxious moments when the drivers had to restart the cars after pit stops.

In the Grand Touring category, one of the four 1964 Ferrari GTOs had had its final drive casing disintegrate as it passed the pits, and part of this dented an E-type Jaguar being serviced in the pits. The Cobra Daytona of Gurney and Bondurant, in any case, was faster than the surviving GTOs, and went on to win the class, so Ford had some consolation at least. Among the British teams there were many retirements. The Aston Martin had been disqualified just before ten on the Sunday morning for taking on oil before it had covered the necessary 25 laps. At the time it was lying eleventh. Both works-entered Sunbeam Tigers had also retired. These were a new concoction from Rootes consisting of the Sunbeam Alpine and a 4·2-litre Ford V-8 engine tuned by Shelby but using the standard four-barrel Ford-Carter carburettor. The suspension had been modified by Brian Lister, who used to build Lister sports cars and included extra rear radius arms to take location loads off the springs. Both privately entered E-type Jaguars had also retired. Although weather conditions were fine throughout the race, there was an unexpected and sharp frost during the night and the Maranello Concessionaires 250GTO driven by Innes Ireland and Tony Maggs had to make a pit stop for ice to be cleared from the throttles.

So the race ran out with Ferrari in five out of the first six places and Ford having learned some salutary lessons – the principal one being not to rely on other peoples' gearboxes!

RESULTS

no. of laps

1st	J. Guichet/N. Vaccarella (Ferrari 275/P)	348
	(distance covered 2917·7 miles – 121·55 mph)	
2nd	G. Hill/J. Bonnier (Ferrari 330/P)	343
3rd	J. Surtees/L. Bandini (Ferrari 330/P)	336
4th	D. Gurney/R. Bondurant (A.C. Cobra-Ford)	333
5th	L. Bianchi/'Beurlys' (Ferrari GTO – 1964)	332
6th	I. Ireland/A. Maggs (Ferrari GTO – 1964)	327
7th	R. Buchet/G. Ligier (Porsche 904GTS)	322
8th	B. Pon/V. Zalinge (Porsche 904GTS)	318
9th	F. Tavano/R. Grossman (Ferrari GTO – 1964)	314
10th	G. Koch/H. Schiller (Porsche 904GTS)	314
11th	H. Muller/C. Sage (Porsche 904GTS)	308
12th	'Franc'/J. Kerguen (Porsche 904GTS)	307
13th	R. Businello/B. Deserti (Alfa Romeo GTZ)	306
14th	P. Noblet/E. Berney (Iso Rivolta A3 Grifo)	306
15th	G. Sala/G. Biscaldi (Alfa Romeo GTZ)	304
16th	P. Dumay/G. Langlois (Ferrari 275LM)	297
17th	R. de Lageneste/H. Morrogh (Alpine-Renault)	291
18th	J. de Mortemart/J. Fraissinet (A.C. Cobra-Ford)	288
19th	A. Hedges/P. Hopkirk (MGB)	286
20th	M. Zeccoli/R. Masson (Alpine-Renault)	283
21st	D. Hobbs/R. Slotemaker (Triumph Spitfire)	271
22nd	C. Hunt/J. Wagstaff (Lotus Elite)	265
23rd	S. Lelong/P. Farjon (René-Bonnet)	259
24th	C. Baker/W. Bradley (Austin-Healey Sprite)	256
25th	M. Bianchi/J. Vinatier (Alpine-Renault)	229

The Guichet/Vaccarella Ferrari also won the Index of Performance

The Rheims 12-hours race

As the French Grand Prix was held at Rouen, and only a week after Le Mans, the Automobile Club de Champagne decided to attract spectator interest by reviving the 12-hours sports car race which had last been held in 1958 and then for Grand Touring cars only, as well as staging Formula Two and Three events. The Formula Two and Three races were a hoot for everyone except the entrants, who had to foot the bills for blown-up engines, for the top speed of even the Formula Two cars was only approximately the same as the average lap speed of the quicker prototypes on this very fast circuit and so the single-seaters were going round flat out all the way except for braking hard for the two hairpin bends. Like almost all racing circuits in France, Rheims-Geux is made up of public roads and anyone travelling into Rheims along the N.31 (it is easily recognisable by the Dunlop bridge straddling the road) will appreciate the sort of speeds that can be obtained.

The 12-hours race was much more successful, even though Ferrari did not enter any works cars, for he had decided to withdraw from prototype racing until 1965 so that he could concentrate his efforts on the Grand Prix scene. Although only a fortnight had elapsed since Le Mans, Ford had endeavoured to sort out their transmission problems and were just hoping that the Colotti units would hold together for a race that lasted only half as long as the Le Mans event. The gearboxes had been fitted with new selectors and very carefully hardened dog-rings. The two pairs, Hill/McLaren and Ginther/Gregory, had their Le Mans cars, but Attwood and Schlesser had a brand new car, the fifth to be built, and on this occasion powered by a 4·7-litre Shelby-tuned iron block production engine instead of the Indianapolis unit.

Despite the absence of Works Ferraris, there was a strong contingent of works-assisted private owners:

Maranello Concessionaires:
275LM driven by Graham Hill and Joakim Bonnier (the bearded Swede, who is President of the Grand Prix Drivers' Association, was one of the most experienced drivers in the race and had been in International racing for ten years)
North American Racing Team:
275LM driven by John Surtees and Lorenzo Bandini
Ecurie Francorchamps:
275LM driven by Langlois van Ophem and 'Beurlys'

Backing up these prototypes, Maranello Concessionaires had a 250GTO, while NART had entered two. One of the NART entries was to be particularly closely watched as it was to be handled by two of the fastest Ferrari drivers, Pedro Rodriguez and Nino Vaccarella, the Sicilian lawyer to whom experience was bringing the skill to match his forcefulness. This car should have been driven by the American Skip Hudson, but he was rendered *hors de combat* by having his finger in the door of Luigi Chinetti's touring Ferrari when somebody closed it. There should also have been a 275LM for Jochen Rindt and Umberto Maglioli, but Maglioli had pranged the car in an Italian hill climb.

Among the other entries were the two E-type Jaguars, two Daytona Shelby coupés, the 5-litre Maserati, a Chevrolet Corvette-engined Iso Grifo of beautiful lines and negligible performance that had run at Le Mans, the works Porsche 904s and the long-awaited rear-engined 2½-litre ATS coupé entered by Stirling Moss' former mechanic, Alf Francis. The ATS, alas, did not make the start line. While being towed back to its quarters after a practice breakdown it was rammed up the back by a Peugeot 404.

As a prelude to 17 hours of almost non-stop racing (including the single-seater races) the organisers allowed the drivers an easy time, with three days of practice and a day of rest before the 12-hours race started at midnight on the Saturday. As practice did not start until 4 pm, continuing until 10 pm, the more indolent drivers could take it really easy, swimming or sunning themselves at the pool at the Parc Pommery. After practice was over, the drivers would settle down to the serious business of the day with a late dinner and heavy training for the all-night stint on Sunday at one of the better bars in Rheims area. Despite the presence of the Fords, which were generally reckoned to have the legs of the Ferraris, Surtees with the Maranello 275LM was fastest in practice with a time of 2 min 19·2 sec (133·4 mph), fractionally faster than Ginther and McLaren with a time of 2 min 20 sec and 2 min 20·3 sec respectively. As there were only 37 starters, speed differential between the cars was not as big a worry as it might have been, but a lot of people were worried about what might happen when the field was unleashed at midnight with the faster cars reaching speeds of over 170 mph and the drivers not having a chance to acclimatise themselves to the dark.

At midnight, when the drivers were lined up in the floodlit area at the start, Tito Roche dropped the flag unexpectedly quickly. First away was the 904 Porsche of Jo Siffert, but he was pushed off the narrow road as the faster boys elbowed their way to the front. A fantastic high-speed traffic jam swept under the Dunlop Bridge and when the glare of the headlamps of the leading cars merged with the floodlit pit area at the end of the first lap, Graham Hill's 275LM held a tenuous lead over the Fords of Ginther and McLaren, who in turn led Surtees' Ferrari. Surtees passed McLaren, and all the way round the circuit during the ensuing laps the three leaders swapped places furiously, passing each other, running in line, running three abreast, lapping the slowest cars, sometimes one on each side, sometimes thrusting themselves down the middle between a pair of stragglers. They screamed along the narrow track past the pits at around 160 mph, and were taking the fast curves of the circuit almost flat out. As they crested the rises on the circuit their headlamps pointed into the sky, while the road beyond was blind. Ginther's Ford was slightly faster along the straights, but the 5-speed gearbox of the Ferraris gave them an advantage on acceleration. Each driver was confident not only of his own ability to lap Rheims in the dark at speeds close to 130 mph, but confident also of the ability of the other two drivers. Disaster, however, struck on lap 8, for as Jean Beltoise with a René-Bonnet was being lapped by the leaders he panicked, lost control, and went off the road. Beltoise escaped with a broken arm, although the car was burnt out. As a result of this incident McLaren fell back slightly and started to lap at a rather slower rate than the two leaders.

By the end of the first hour's racing the leaders had completed 24 laps, McLaren was now 40 seconds in arrears and Attwood with the third Ford a further 20 seconds back. On lap 30, Ginther put in a time of 2 min 20 sec, but four laps later stopped at the Thillois hairpin with a broken crown wheel and pinion. Not long afterwards McLaren came in to refuel, but 19 minutes were lost while the clutch return spring was replaced and Hill rejoined the race with this car in 24th place. Shortly after 4 am Schlesser made an unscheduled pit stop with his Ford which was now in third place. A gearbox plug had fallen out; this was rectified and the car rejoined the race, but retired almost at once as the loss of oil had damaged the transmission. A bare half-hour had elapsed when the sole remaining Ford driven by Hill gave a loud bang as it passed the pits, and shortly afterwards Hill returned to the pits on foot. Although the engine had blown up and everybody knew it, the official reason for retirement given by

Ford was gearbox trouble. An additional failing of the Fords which revealed itself at this race was overheating of the brake discs and these were red hot for the whole time the cars were running. Eleven years previously Jaguars had had exactly the same trouble with their Dunlop disc brakes on the XK 120C – no bothers at Le Mans (which they won) but red hot discs in the Goodwood 9-hours race.

If the leading Ferraris had been works cars, they would have eased off the pace to be certain of keeping the race in their pockets, but as it was British Concessionaire versus American Concessionaire the battle continued unabated. The Surtees/Bandini car of NART led the Hill/Bonnier car of Maranello by a minute at 5 am, and at 7 am Surtees set a new fastest lap of 2 min 19·6 sec (about 133 mph). During the night, several of the Ferrari 250GTOs had suffered from carburettor icing, but none of the rear-engined cars had this trouble. The Maserati went out with a recurrence of its Le Mans electrical trouble and the Belgian 275LM had been eliminated by crown wheel and pinion failure.

Seconds lost or gained in the pits were playing a vital part in this battle between the leading Ferraris and on Sunday morning both cars needed a tyre change. Although otherwise identical cars, this incident highlighted a difference between them. The NART car was understeering and needed its left-hand front tyre changing, whereas the Maranello car, which was oversteering, had worn out its left-hand rear tyre. In addition, both cars needed brake pad changes, but on modern competition cars, this consumes but a few seconds. Shortly before 10 am the NART car had stopped to refuel, but while it was stopped Graham Hill went into the lead. His last fuel stop was due shortly and he endeavoured to gain as much ground as possible, in the process setting a new lap record of 2 min 19·2 sec. Hill made his stop and handed over to Bonnier, but Surtees realised that he was running out of brake pads and a hasty stop was made to change these. At 11 am, with one hour's racing left, it was realised that Surtees would pass Bonnier in about ten minutes. Shortly afterwards Surtees went missing and eventually limped round to the pits with a flat left-hand front tyre. This time the race was lost and, he restarted over a lap behind Bonnier. Although Surtees continued at unabated speed, it was a hopeless chase and he had to be content with second place.

The Rheims race displayed how well placed was Ferrari's faith in the private owners who ran his cars, but it also indicated that the

275LM was a car of tremendous speed and reliability. After twelve hours of racing the leadings cars, despite having been driven flat out in their efforts to beat the Fords and each other, were in superb mechanical condition, and had received no mechanical attention of any kind.

The Tourist Trophy

Britain's oldest motor race, although still a fine event, was but a shadow of its former self. Held first in the Isle of Man and then at Ards and on the Dundrod circuit in Northern Ireland, it had flourished as Britain's only race to be held on closed public roads, but had been transferred to Goodwood after the 1955 race, in which crashes cost the lives of four drivers. In September 1964 it was held over 130 laps of the 2·4-mile circuit and was for sports and prototype sports cars over 1600 cc and Grand Touring cars over 2000 cc. Although not attracting the important entries seen in the Continental races apart from Shelby's Cobras, in 1964 Graham Hill was entered by Maranello Concessionaires in a 330/P and David Piper had his new Ferrari 275LM. After the retirement of McLaren's Cooper-Oldsmobile and Jim Clark in a works Lotus 30 Ford sports/racing car, Hill won by a little over a lap from Piper. It was not an exciting race, but it was another display of Ferrari reliability.

The Paris 1000 Kilometres Race

Although an event counting towards the Prototype and Grand Touring Championships, the race on the banked Montlhéry track just outside Paris attracted little in the way of works entries. There were no works Ferraris, because Ferrari had already had a clear victory in the Prototype category, no Fords, because Ford had nothing to gain by another defeat and wanted to concentrate on sorting out their cars for the 1965 season, and no Cobras, because Shelby had already gained clear victory in the Grand Touring category.

The honour of Maranello rested on the strong entry of privately owned Ferraris. The Swiss Scuderia Filipinetti had entered two 275LMs, while from Maranello Concessionaires there was a 330/P for Graham Hill and the Swedish driver Joakim Bonnier, and a 275LM for Jackie Stewart and Scarfiotti. The Équipe Nationale

Belge 275LM was driven by 'Beurlys' and Willy Mairesse, a former works Ferrari driver who was making a return to racing after a crash in 1963 at the German Grand Prix with a Ferrari.

Right from the start the 330/P, without doubt the fastest car in the race, shot into the lead and put an enormous amount of ground between itself and the Maranello 275LM in second spot. These positions were unchanged at half-distance, but soon afterwards Jackie Stewart with the second place car lost six laps while a broken steering arm was replaced. He rejoined the race only to be confronted by two of the smaller cars spinning in his path; to avoid them he had to spin too, and the result was that the Ferrari suffered a severely crumpled rear end.

Shortly afterwards a serious accident occurred in front of the pits. Lindner, the German Jaguar concessionaire and an enthusiastic driver seen at the most important Continental races, lost control of his competition E-type and smashed straight into Franco Patria's Abarth-Simca 1300 which was waiting to rejoin the race after a pit stop. Both cars were completely wrecked, the Jaguar finishing up some 150 yards further down the track. Patria was killed instantly, Lindner died shortly afterwards in hospital and, in addition, the incident cost the lives of three flag marshals.

For the remainder of the race there were no changes in the positions of the leading cars, and Hill and Bonnier completed the 129 laps ahead of a GTO entered by NART and driven by Pedro Rodriguez and Jo Schlesser. After its alarms and excursions the other Maranello car, the 275LM of Stewart and Scarfiotti, was tenth. In 7th place came the first British car, the modified competition E-type of Dick Protheroe co-driving with John Coundley. This special-bodied and very beautiful E-type is still driven in British hill climbs, and with considerable success, by Mike Wright.

The 1964 season had seen the continued domination of prototype racing by Ferrari, but as much through the efforts of private teams as the works. Both the private teams who had done so well, Maranello Concessionaires and the North American Racing Team, had raced with works support and were often loaned cars by the works. This diversification of entries was one of the many lessons learned by Ford and which they would apply as part of their renewed effort for the 1965 season.

Above: For 1965, Ford developed the Mark II cars powered by 7-litre engines and two of these ran at Le Mans in June. Both retired and this car, driven by Ken Miles and Bruce McLaren, was eliminated by gearbox trouble. *Below:* Among other entries in the 1965 race was this 4·7-litre open car entered by Ford France and driven by Maurice Trintignant and Guy Ligier. These cars were developed by John Wyer in England and their only advantage was a slight reduction in weight

John Surtees, who led the Ferrari team until his disagreement with team manager Dragoni in 1966

The most successful Italian driver in recent years was the late Lorenzo Bandini, seen here with team-mate Chris Amon who joined the Ferrari team for the 1967 season

SEVEN
1965

Ford Developments

The most notable change to the Ford organisation was the departure of Eric Broadley, who was relieved to find himself independent and was able to open his new works at Slough. Although it was not to be eligible as a Grand Touring prototype until 1967, Broadley was at work on a new project, a Chevrolet-powered sports car that was to be even more advanced in design than the Ford GT.

Ford had made the decision to split their racing activities. While John Wyer, as Managing Director of Ford Advanced Vehicles Ltd, was to continue being responsible for the development of the existing car and, in due course, to build a production batch of them, a contract was placed with Carroll Shelby to prepare the cars that would represent the main thrust of the Ford attack in 1965. A third course of action was the formation in late 1964 of the fresh Ford-controlled set-up at Kar-Kraft, a new Ford racing subsidiary at Detroit.

At Shelby American, the team of Shelby himself, Phil Remington his chief engineer and Ken Miles, who was Shelby's test driver and competition adviser, concentrated on improvements both in the interests of greater performance and greater reliability, for it was clear that Ferrari would answer the Ford challenge with an even faster car. It was decided to scrap the Indianapolis 4·2-litre engine and substitute the 4·7-litre cast iron production engine used in the Cobra. Although this was rather heavier than the 4·2, it had the excellent output of 385 bhp and its greater torque was an advantage with the four-speed gearbox that would still be used. In an attempt to overcome the gearbox troubles that had plagued the cars during 1964, certain of the Colotti straight-cut gears were replaced by

Ford-made helical gears. In all, 21 changes were made to the transmission unit.

A reversion was made to the cast alloy wheels as originally used on the Lola and the flow of cooling air to the brakes, engine and gearbox was improved. It was also decided to use Goodyear tyres of greater diameter than the original Dunlops. Other changes of a detailed nature were made to the drive-shafts, the fuel feed system and the clutch.

At Kar-Kraft Roy Lunn was engaged on an even more ambitious version of the GT40 which was to be known as the Mk II. Lunn realised that by modifying the seating position and the rear bulkhead members it would be possible to slip into the chassis the 7-litre Ford Galaxie engine which in tuned form had been successful in American saloon car racing. By normal competition standards, and certainly by Ferrari's, this was a brutal and rather unsophisticated way of gaining extra power. For, like the 4·7-litre unit, this was basically a typically American cast-iron pushrod V-8 – but as used in the GT40 with a power output of 475 bhp. Even so, the unit's efficiency is low, approximately 70 bhp per litre as compared with the now commonplace 100 bhp. It is also a heavy engine, weighing close to 600 lb. Modifications included a single four-barrel carburettor, dry sump lubrication and aluminium cylinder heads. Its maximum power output was developed at only 6200 rpm and it possessed the fantastic torque of some 475 lb/ft at only 4000 rpm. This meant a really usable and wide power band and the need only for a four-speed transmission.

To develop the Mk II, built up cars were shipped from Slough for installation of the engine and detail work in the States. One serious problem was the development of a transmission unit that would be capable of taking all that extra power with reliability. The answer was found to lie in enclosing the gears and shafts from the Galaxie saloon in a light alloy casing. A larger radiator and a remote oil tank were installed at the front of the car and the front and rear body structures were modified.

While the 4·7-litre cars were being put through their paces in April at the Le Mans practice week-end, the first of the Mk IIs was being tested at Ford's own proving ground at Michigan. It was found that the car was able to lap the circuit there at 201·5 mph and it exceeded 210 mph along the straights. The Mk II then went to the Riverside Raceway in California, where it completed a 24-hour reliability run without mechanical failure. Ford engineers were able to calculate from these tests that the Mk II would be able to lap Le Mans at between 3 min 30 sec and 3 min 35 sec compared with the record lap set by Hill's Ford in the 1964 race of 3 min 49 sec. A decision, as it later proved a wrong decision, was made to rush the preparation of two of these cars through in time for Le Mans, now a bare two months away.

Ferrari Developments

At Maranello Ferrari was concentrating on improvements to his prototypes and once again was racing two sizes of car, although technically they were very similar. The first of these was the 330/P2, with an engine of 3967 cc developing 410 bhp at 8200 rpm and the other was the 275/P2 with a capacity of 3286 cc and a power output of 350 bhp at 8500 rpm. These engine sizes were the same as used in 1964, with six Weber twin-choke carburettors and twin plugs per cylinder, but there were now twin overhead camshafts per bank of cylinders. The chassis of the two cars were very similar with wishbones and coil spring front suspension, and at the rear a lower wishbone, combined coil spring and damper unit, a top transverse strut and double radius rods. These cars ran on the latest wide-tread Dunlop tyres, and to fit these Ferrari was using a new 15 in cast alloy wheel made to Dunlop specification in his own foundry. Although these cars had, strictly speaking, open bodywork, with the high regulation windscreen and the 'boom' running across the car behind the cockpit they were almost coupés.

Ferrari was none too keen on letting the private teams who support him so well have the new four-cam engine, so as a sop he provided an enlarged version of the 330/P engine with a capacity of 4390 cc (81 × 71 mm) and developing 380 bhp at 7300 rpm. At the Le Mans test day in April, one of the 4·4 cars owned by the Swiss Scuderia Filipinetti team and driven by the unknown Swiss driver Tommy Spychiger was lapping almost as fast as the works cars.

Still unable to get the 275LM homologated as a Grand Touring car, Ferrari had produced a lightweight competition version of his new production car, the 275GTB. This car was a vast improvement on the 250GTO and as well as featuring a 5-speed gearbox in unit with the final drive and the enlarged 3·3-litre engine, there was independent rear suspension and cast alloy wheels. As something like 135 of the production cars had been built when the 275GTB was put forward for homologation, it looked as if there would be no snags. Unfortunately for Enzo, Carroll Shelby drew attention to the great weight discrepancy between the quoted weight of the production car and the actual weight of the competition version. There would have been no objection to a slight difference, as a competition version would be expected to be one or two hundredweight lighter than its road counterpart, but the difference between the Ferraris was quite unacceptable. Ferrari's immediate reaction was that he would not allow works GT cars to take part in Championship events. This did not worry anyone a great deal except the lucky teams who were in the habit of being loaned a works car, and it delighted Shelby, who could see the Grand Touring Championship as a Cobra push-over.

Daytona Continental

The Daytona race had graduated from the Grand Touring event of the previous two years to a 2000 kilometre race for sports cars as well as Grand Touring cars and prototypes. Although Ferrari did not enter, he loaned NART and John Mecom two of the latest 330/P2s, while two of the re-worked Fords made their debut under the Shelby banner. Neither of these makes set the pace, however, and for two-thirds of the race the leader was the very fragile Ford V-8-powered Lotus of Dan Gurney and Jerry Grant, which romped away from the rest of the field until eliminated by engine trouble. By this time both the thinly-disguised works Ferraris had fallen by the wayside with transmission trouble. The race had taken heavy toll of the entrants in mechanical failures and the Ford GT of Ken Miles and Lloyd Ruby scored the model's first, unexpected, but comparatively easy victory. The next car home was a Cobra coupé five laps in arrears and the other Ford finished third – but 28 laps behind the winner after mechanical troubles.

Sebring

Once again Ferrari did not enter works cars in the Sebring 12-hours race but NART and Mecom reappeared with the same two cars that had run at Daytona. Neither these nor the two Ford GTs were, however, the sensation of the meeting, for all eyes were focussed on the Chaparrals, sponsored and driven by Texas oilman Jim Hall. These cars had been running in American sports car events for two seasons, and although it was an open secret in United States racing circles that General Motors dropped Hall large sums of money on the quiet to help in developing and racing them, it was the first occasion on which they achieved prominence. Powering the Chaparral was a very special 5·4-litre Chevrolet engine (as usual, a V-8), and they used a 'hush-hush' form of 2-speed automatic transmission. At this stage in the Chaparral's career it was not known how the transmission worked, and certainly not appreciated that it worked so well. The young Texan was rather shy about the whole project and if anyone asked him leading questions about the Chaparral's engine or transmission, he smiled and said nothing.

In a sense he did not need to say anything, for in practice the Chaparral spoke for itself. Hall lapped the Sebring circuit in 2 min 57·6 sec (105·9 mph) which cut 9 seconds off John Surtees' 1964 lap record with a Ferrari. Hall's team-mate managed 3 minutes dead and the next fastest cars, the GT40s of McLaren and Ginther, were 7 and 8·3 seconds slower. The Chaparral's reliability was, however, unproved, and it was generally considered an outsider.

As testimony of the interest taken by the American public in sports car racing, the roads to the circuit were jammed with traffic from 6 am onwards. While the crowds were entertained by the Sebring High School band and the antics of its corps of majorettes, who may have a certain sex appeal to the American male but to European eyes are redolent of hygienic sterility, the drivers kept out of the blazing sunshine and anxiously awaited the start. Sixty-seven drivers lined up for the Le Mans-type start, and when the green starting flag fell Richie Ginther's Ford led the field. At the end of the first lap he came into the pits for the removal of a stone which had jammed the front brake caliper. The battle for the lead was now between Dan Gurney's Lotus 19 and the Chaparral of Hall. By lap 5 Gurney and Hall had a lead of 17 seconds over the other Chaparral, which was tailed by Rodriguez' Ferrari and Miles' Ford. So the race continued at this hot pace until the first change of drivers. When Hall made his pit stop, Gurney went into the lead.

After the Chaparral re-started, Hap Sharp started to close up on the tiring Gurney, but the shape of the race changed dramatically and unexpectedly. Phil Hill, who had taken over the Ford from Ginther, was forced to abandon his vain chase of the leaders when the Ford fractured a spring mounting and soon afterwards Gurney was forced to pull off the road when the fuel pump drive failed. While the Hall/Sharp Chaparral continued to build up its lead, its team-mate driven by Hissom and Jennings was in and out of the pit with electrical trouble and gradually fell to the tail of the field. In second place was the John Mecom-entered Ferrari of Graham Hill and Pedro Rodriguez, and third the remaining Ford.

The air-temperature had reached an energy-sapping 97 degrees, while the oil-stained, rubber-coated track was a blistering 130 degrees. Just after 4 pm, when the Chaparral had a 6-lap lead, ominous thunder could be heard in the distance and the sky became enveloped with the black threat of a storm. When or how hard it was likely to rain was uncertain, and when cars came in for their routine pit-stops, nobody could make up their minds whether to fit rain tyres or not. At 5.25 pm, by when the Chaparral's lead was $7\frac{1}{2}$ laps, came the outburst. Solid sheets of almost opaque rain slammed on to the circuit. Huge pools of water formed on the track and a raging torrent swept through the pit area, carrying away signalling gear and spare wheels. The drivers in the open cars sat in a bath of water, visibility was nil, speeds fell to below 30 mph and the bow-waves set up by the cars made the event look like a power-boat race. The works Porsche team were pressing on to narrow the gap between themselves and the big-bangers, who were affected far more by the conditions and an Iso Grifo, the driver completely blinded, slammed into the Mercedes-Benz Bridge over the track and was cut in two. In the pits, things were little better. Mechanics sometimes found themselves waist-deep in water and a Cobra mechanic was found unconscious in a large pool – he had received an electric shock from an exposed power cable.

The rain lasted for an hour, with the heavier cars spending more time in the pits than on the track – it is doubtful whether the leading Chaparral covered more than two laps in this time. By 7 pm, while most of the field were still spluttering round with electrical and ignition trouble, the timekeepers had sorted themselves out and it became clear that the smaller cars had been too far behind to make any impression on the leaders and the Chaparral still had a 4-lap lead over the second-place Ferrari. The Ferrari did not last long, however, for its clutch burnt out – when Rodriguez handed over to Hill he forgot to mention the clutch trouble and Graham thought he was getting excessive wheelspin! At 9 pm, to the sound of horns and wild (if somewhat nasal) cheering, Jim Hall brought his Chaparral home to its first important victory – and its last for a long time to come. In second place was the Ford of McLaren and Miles, giving a demonstration of the reliability that Ford appeared to have found at the expense of speed. One of the interesting sidelights of the race was that the winning car did not score any points towards the Championship as the FIA classified it as a sports car rather than a Grand Touring prototype.

The Le Mans Test Week-end

The Le Mans test week-end in April saw the first European appearance of the new Ferraris, and the Ford teams were out in force. As well as the Shelby team with rather tatty-looking blue cars, John Wyer was at the Sarthe circuit with an open version of the GT as well as two of the familiar blue-and-white coupés. This open car was also fitted with a ZF gearbox in place of the original Colotti unit. One of the Shelby cars was tried with a longer and better profiled snout which screwed over the existing nose. It was driven by Bondurant who found it unstable at high speed.

The open version of the GT40 was John Wyer's own creation and although Ford persevered with open cars for almost a year their advantage was negligible. The open car was lighter, but drivers preferred the coupés, which were in any case aerodynamically better, for a number of good reasons. Generally drivers found the coupé more comfortable, as they were well protected from the elements, they were quieter than the open cars and accordingly less tiring in a long-distance race, and they were more than adequately ventilated. This in itself highlighted two more of the important developments in sports car racing which had occurred unobtrusively. There had been a vogue during the years 1952–3 for enclosed coupés, and these were raced at Le Mans by Mercedes-Benz, Alfa Romeo, Bristol, Lancia, Ferrari and Cunningham. The two major snags with these cars had been the designing of windscreen wipers that would prove effective at high speeds and the fact that these starkly-trimmed enclosed coupés tended to work as resonance boxes, amplifying road and engine noise to an unbearable degree. Most people therefore raced open cars, and the aero screens did not need windscreen wipers. When the FIA prescribed a minimum windscreen height, constructors had to evolve wipers that would work at high speeds.

Similarly, developments had taken place in keeping the noise level down and, in any case, the problem was less acute with a rear-engined car.

Another toy with which John Wyer was playing was a King Cobra with the 4·7-litre engine. The King Cobra was another Shelby project which sold in small numbers for sports car racing in the States, and was basically the rear-engined Cooper-Monaco sports car of 1959 fitted with the Ford engine and brought up-to-date with a few modifications. As well as seeing whether there was anything to be learnt from the car that would help with Ford development, Wyer entered it for Roy Salvadori to drive at Goodwood and in the Tourist Trophy, which had been transferred to Oulton Park, Britain's most beautiful racing circuit, and was held in May. It turned up to both events looking rather tatty and failed to start on either occasion.

The Monza 1000 kilometres Race

On 25th April a new event was held at Monza, a late addition to the calendar by the Italians and a very convenient one for Enzo Ferrari, who had not run in either of the American events. So that a large number of runners could be accommodated, the Monza authorities used the full 10-kilometre circuit which took in the concrete bankings. These have a very rough surface and so, to prevent the faster prototypes hitting this at close to 180 mph, which might well have caused structural failures, artificial corners were added in before the south banking. Even so, there were a large number of failures of such components as steering and suspension.

The star of the meeting was undoubtedly the new Ferrari Dino prototype which Enzo hoped would eventually form the basis for a Fiat production car and could be homologated in the Grand Touring category. It was also intended that sufficient cars should be produced to satisfy the new Formula Two regulations which were to come into force for the 1967 season. This limited power units to series production units of 1600 cc of which not less than 50 had been produced. When the Fiat eventually entered production, it was front-engined. Ferrari built in 1967 a Formula Two car powered by this unit, but he has made no serious attempts either to develop or race it. The heart of the Dino prototype was a V-6 four overhead camshaft engine of 1592 cc similar in most respects to the unit used in the Ferrari Grand Prix car of the 1961 season. This engine, developing 196 bhp, was

Discussing 1965 Le Mans prospects are Carroll Shelby (left of picture) who has been responsible for the preparation of the most successful Ford cars, and Phil Hill. Hill was a works Ferrari driver, and at the wheel of Maranello cars won the 1961 Grand Prix Drivers' World Championship. After a spell with Fords, he is now in the Chaparral team

The driver who has probably covered more miles in Ford GTs than all the other drivers put together, Bruce McLaren, who has been responsible for much of the development testing of these cars

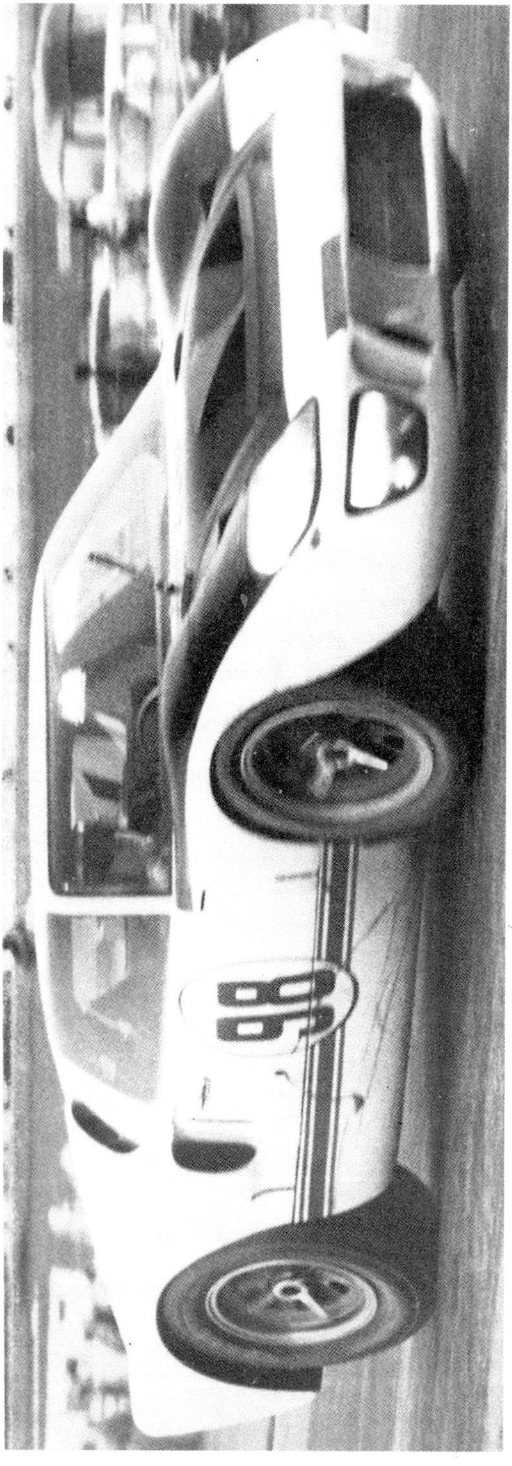

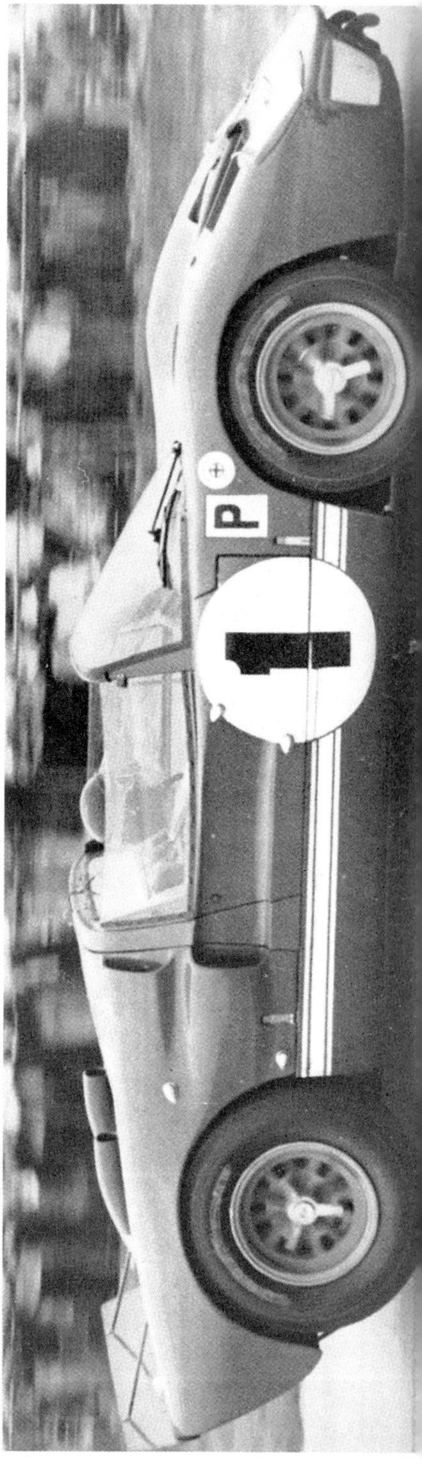

mounted at the rear of a Grand Prix type chassis with double wishbones and coil spring front and rear suspension. A very pretty Farina coupé body was fitted and the car looked a formidable challenger in its class, but its Monza debut was disappointing, as it retired with engine trouble on the very first lap.

At Monza, Enzo Ferrari fielded three potential winners; two of these were the 4-litre 330/P2 and were driven by John Surtees/ Lodovico Scarfiotti and Lorenzo Bandini/Nino Vaccarella, while a 3·3-litre car was given to Mike Parkes and Jean Guichet. Ferrari's hand was strengthened by the presence of a Maranello Concesionaires 330/P driven by Joakim Bonnier and David Piper, who had left his own 275LM at home, and the Scuderia Filipinetti 4-litre model which had shown itself nearly as fast as the works cars at the Le Mans test day. Ford had turned up with two cars under Shelby's wing, and these were driven by Bruce McLaren/Ken Miles and Chris Amon/Umberto Maglioli.

A flying start was used and the cars did a lap behind a course car before being released by the starter's flag half-way along the pit straight. At the end of the first lap Surtees led from Bandini, Parkes, Müller (Filipinetti 4·4), McLaren, Mairesse (Ecurie Francorchamps 275LM), Bonnier, Amon and Innes Ireland (Maranello 275LM). In the next few laps there were no changes except that Bonnier managed to squeeze past Mairesse, but the bumpy surface of the banking soon started to play havoc and the first of many retirements occurred. Mairesse came in with steering trouble, rejoined the race, but eventually retired with this trouble. Suspension failure eliminated Bandini on lap 9, Surtees was delayed by a puncture, as were Ireland and Bonnier. To cap all these Ferrari troubles, Tommy Spychiger who had taken over the Filipinetti car, failed to slow for the Parabola bend, a slow second-gear corner with a high-speed approach, the car left the track, plunged through the trees, killing the driver.

Out at the front was the 275/P2 of Parkes and Guichet which at 50 laps, the half-way mark, had averaged 125·9 mph. Surtees had worked his way back to second place and the Fords were lying third and fourth. The positions of the three leaders remained unchanged till the finish, but the second Ford of Amon and Maglioli retired with collapsed front suspension. Although Fords had now finished in a European race, it appeared that the 4·7-litre car was just not

---

The Mk II version of the GT40 was considerably modified for the 1966 season, and in February one driven by the late Ken Miles and Lloyd Ruby won the Daytona 24-hours race – but no works Ferrari were entered. The following month Ford scored a further victory in the Sebring 12-hours race. The drivers were again Ken Miles and Lloyd Ruby. The car was an open version of the Mk II known as the X-1

fast enough to match the improved Ferraris, for at Monza neither car was ever able to challenge for the lead.

The Targa Florio

The Sicilian event is now perhaps the most nostalgic event on the motor racing calendar, dating back to the turn of the century and retaining many of the features of racing of that era – it is over a lengthy course (a lap amounts to 72 kilometres, approximately 45 miles) and it is held on tortuous, mountainous, dusty, rock-strewn roads. Although the organisers no longer have to worry about the local banditry taking pot-shots at the drivers, any driver who abandons his car after a breakdown is likely to incur the wrath of his team manager; for by the time the car is recovered the more easily removable components are likely to have been carried off by the local peasants – unless of course the car belongs to one of their favourites, such as Nino Vaccarella. Vaccarella, who is a professor of Law in Palermo, is probably the only local driver to have made the top grade in International sports car racing, and therefore the only driver of a potential winner with a really intimate knowledge of the course. With such a long circuit, and two drivers per car, a driver is lucky indeed to get more than one practice lap in the time allotted. With such a large proportion of the drivers not knowing on many occasions which way the road goes, it is hardly surprising that there are so many crashes – a cause and effect which also made the famous Mille Miglia so dangerous. The local inhabitants regard the Targa Floria as a national festival, and display their partisanship to drivers and teams with home-made banners and whitewashed signs on the road and walls of buildings. Of course the local blue-eyed boy is Vaccarella, and such signs as 'Forza Vaccarella' and 'Viva Ferrari' are to be seen at every inhabited place on the course.

Ferrari turned up in force to support the 1965 race and entered three of his latest 330/P2s shared by Vaccarella and Bandini, Scarfiotti and Parkes, and Guichet and Baghetti. In addition there was a full competition 275GTB for Biscaldi and Deserti and the promising young Italian driver, bespectacled Andreas de Adamich had been loaned a 275LM by the works, and this he shared with Casona. There were a total of four 275LMs entered and out of deference to Ferrari's views on the refusal to homologate the model, a special National class to accommodate these cars was provided.

Facing the full might of Maranello was the usual strong Porsche team of four cars, consisting of two cars with the flat 8-cylinder engine, a coupé and an open car, the third, one of the familiar flat-six coupés powered by a more highly-tuned version of the engine used in the production 911 model, and finally a 904GTS coupé.

The 1964 race had discouraged Shelby from turning up to the Targa Florio and the sole Ford entry was John Wyer's open car which had now been painted green and was driven by Sir John Whitmore and Bob Bondurant. In the Targa Florio it is not really possible to drive in a really scientific manner, lining the car up precisely for every corner and estimating braking and gearchange points within a matter of a yard or so, as most drivers do not know the circuit well enough. Nor is it possible to drive with a great deal of discretion and care, as you will then not be going fast enough to figure in the results. The best a driver can hope for is to press on fiercely and hopefully, relying on his experience to get him out of difficulties. Both Whitmore and Bondurant were admirably suited to this type of driving. British entries in the race were confined to a Vitafoam Racing Team - entered Sunbeam Tiger, a works Austin Healey 3000 and Sprite, an MGB and a Dick Jacobs-entered Midget.

At 8 am the first of the 59 starters left Cerda with the rest of the field following at 30-second intervals. The weather was oppressively hot and the roads exceedingly dusty. On his second lap, Vaccarella lapped at 39 min 21 sec, which bettered the existing three-year-old lap record by 39 seconds, and he appeared to have the race in his pocket, provided that Bandini would be able to keep up the lap times when his turn at the wheel came. On the third lap Scarfiotti went off the road and damaged the steering and four laps later Baghetti's Ferrari had its battery disintegrate leaving him without ignition and he was forced to abandon the car.

The real hard-luck story of the race, though, was that of Ford. After suffering in the early stages of the race from a mis-firing engine, the car started to run well. Then, on the third lap, as Whitmore was pressing on down the straight, the left-hand front wheel came off, bounced off the road and demolished the overhead wires of the main electric railway line. Whitmore fitted the spare wheel, replaced the wheel nut which a policeman had found for him, and limped back to the pits. Four laps later, Bondurant lost control on some gravel, bounced off a wall and tore off the front suspension and a wheel on a water trough. The 275LM of de Adamich also had battery trouble and the works 275GTB was pranged. So only one Ferrari finished, but won, whereas all four of the works Porsches completed the course and occupied the next four places. Whose race morally? – without doubt the German team's, for not only had it survived intact the most dangerous race of the season, but the second place car of Colin Davis and Gerhardt Mitter was only four minutes behind the winner with an engine of 2-litres capacity. Of the British cars, the Healey 3000, the Sprite and the Midget were each second in their class, but the smaller British cars had completed only nine of the ten laps.

Racing at Spa

The Grand Prix de Spa, held over a distance of 500 kilometres the following week-end, attracted entries from neither Ford nor Ferrari, but Mike Parkes turned up to represent his boss with the 330/P of Maranello Concessionaires and there were 275LMs driven by David Piper (his own bright green car) and Willy Mairesse (with the Ecurie Francorchamps car). Parkes romped away from the rest of the field until his refuelling stop on lap 17, when the car was delayed for nearly four minutes while the mechanics sorted out fuel pump trouble. As this race, despite its distance, took the form of a flat out sprint, all hopes of victory were dashed and the race went to the 275LMs, the yellow leading the green.

The Nurbürgring 1000 Kilometres Race

As Ford were concentrating their efforts on Le Mans, their European entries in the early part of the season were rather half-hearted, with the result that Ferrari was nearly always having things very much his own way. At the Nurbürgring the set-up was rather disorganised and Fords appeared under three different banners:

- R. Attwood/J. Whitmore (open car) entered by Ford Advanced Vehicles (green)
- P. Hill/B. McLaren (5·3-litre enlarged engine) entered by Shelby American
- C. Amon/U. Maglioli entered by Shelby American (both these cars were finished in blue with a white stripe)
- M. Trintignant/G. Ligier entered by Ford-France (white with blue stripes)

Ford-France is the Ford-owned French subsidiary which is purely a marketing company for Ford products in France, and they were running the car on a contractual basis with the parent company. This car was the only one of the Ford entries to retain the wire wheels as seen on the 1964 cars.

Once again Ferrari was in complete command of the situation, and in practice and the race there was no one to match the speed of John Surtees in the 330/P2 who was admirably backed up by his co-driver Scarfiotti. As a second string, Ferrari had entered a 275/P2 3·3-litre car for Mike Parkes and Jean Guichet. Ronnie Hoare of Maranello Concessionaires had twisted Ferrari's arm and had managed to borrow a similar car which was entrusted to BRM team drivers Graham Hill and Jackie Stewart. With this sort of machinery, drivers and pits work that was as good as that of the works, Hoare was in a position to take on and beat the best of the opposition, and beat them he frequently did.

The 1965 Nurbürg race, alas, was not one of those occasions, for while, on lap 10, John Surtees was leading the field, Graham Hill came walking down to the pits from the Maranello car which had expired out on the circuit with electrical failure. Phil Hill's Ford lasted for an even shorter time and expired on the seventh lap when a drive-shaft broke. The decision to use the 5·3-litre engine was an expedient to find more power, but Fords found themselves in a vicious circle as the drive line was no longer strong enough (the 5·3-litre car had already bent one drive shaft in practice).

Shelby decided to call in Amon with the slower of the cars and transfer his two fastest drivers to this. Amon's car had been fluffing round on seven cylinders ever since the start, with everyone in the Shelby pit ignoring it, but even so was in third place. When Amon was given the signal to come in, he did not see it, as he was too busy lapping a slower car to notice, and did a lap too many. The result was that he ran out of fuel just before the pits and had to push the car in. After refuelling, Bruce McLaren took it over, but a lot of time had been lost, and in the confusion everyone forgot that it had been running on seven cylinders. This did not matter, because after a few laps the engine righted itself and McLaren started to lap much faster. While McLaren and Phil Hill were working their way up through the field, Surtees set a new lap record of 8 min 50·5 sec (approximately 96 mph), Parkes with the second place Ferrari gave his pit a few anxious moments when he clouted a car that he was lapping and had to call in at the pits for the bodywork to be bashed clear of the tyre and a wheel change, and the open Ford quietly expired with engine bearer trouble – a fate that also afflicted the Ford-France entry.

While the two leading Ferraris lapped with almost monotonous regularity, attention was focussed on the Dino. After its debacle at Monza, this was regarded as pretty, but rather ineffective. At the Nurbürgring the Dino was a revelation. Driven by Bandini and Vaccarella, it was trouncing the works Porsches on their home territory and led the 2-litre class until it developed a misfire. Bandini brought the Dino into the pits, but the trouble could not be traced, so he continued at reduced speed with the car popping and banging and as a result lost third place and victory in the class to the leading works Porsche. The trouble was subsequently traced to a piece of rubber from a seal in the air intake system being sucked down one of the Webers and partially blocking the jet. Although, as at Monza, the Dino was entered as 1600 cc, it is more than likely that it had the full 2-litre engine which Ferrari announced not long afterwards. At the Nurbürgring this did not matter, as the car was running in the 2-litre class. The surviving Ford finished eighth.

Le Mans

The determination of Ford to win at Le Mans and the determination of Ferrari to retain his domination of the race was apparent in the strength of their entries, for, including Grand Touring cars, there were 11 a side out of 51 starters. Five of the Ford strength lay in Cobras, whereas there was only one Grand Touring Ferrari, a 275GTB entered by the Ecurie Francorchamps. The Ferrari line-up was formed as follows:

Entrant	*Model*	*Drivers*
Works	330/P2	John Surtees/Lodovico Scarfiotti
Works	330/P2	Mike Parkes/Jean Guichet
Works	330/P2	Lorenzo Bandini/Giampero Biscaldi
Maranello Concessionaires	365/P	Joakim Bonnier/David Piper
Maranello Concessionaires	275LM	Lucien Bianchi/Mike Salmon
North American Racing Team	365/P	Pedro Rodriguez/Nino Vaccarella

1965

North American Racing Team	275LM	Masten Gregory/Jochen Rindt
Ecurie Francorchamps	275LM	Langlois van Ophem/'Elde'
Scuderia Filipinetti	275LM	A. Boller/D. Spoerry
Pierre Dumay	275LM	Pierre Dumay/G. Gosselin

The use of the *'nom de course'* by such drivers as 'Elde' and 'Beurlys' who was at the wheel of the 275GTB could be for a variety of reasons. It has been done so that a driver may keep his family in ignorance and prevent them from worrying about him risking his life at Le Mans, or simply because it could be bad for his business if it were known that he was a racing driver. Notable among the Maranello drivers was David Piper, who is among the successful private Ferrari owners. He started racing in 1954 with a pre-war supercharged 750 cc MG with which he was frequently seen in British hill climbs and sprints and graduated through Lotus sports cars to his own Lotus front-engined Grand Prix car. This was plagued with mechanical troubles and he then switched to Ferraris. Ever since he took his Lotus XI sports car all over the Continent in 1956, he has known that it is just about possible, with starting and prize money and bonuses from accessory and tyre manufacturers, to make his racing pay for itself and this is a policy he has followed ever since. Thirty-one-year-old Lucien Bianchi had been steeped in motor racing ever since his childhood. Although an Italian by birth – his father worked in the Alfa Romeo competitions department – he grew up in Belgium, for his father became mechanic to Johnny Claes, who among other cars raced a Grand Prix Lago-Talbot. He had driven privately-entered Ferraris on many occasions and in his role as a garage owner in Brussels had undergone a training course at the Ferrari works.

Leading Ford's challenge were two of the new 7-litre Mk II cars. In a period of five weeks before the race the first car had completed its testing and been rebuilt, while the second had been so hurriedly constructed that it arrived at Le Mans without having turned a wheel under its own power.

The Ford challenge was made up in this way:

Entrant	Model	Drivers
Shelby American Inc.	7-litre Mk II	Ken Miles/Bruce McLaren
Shelby American Inc.	7-litre Mk II	Phil Hill/Chris Amon

Scuderia Filipinetti (prepared by Shelby American)	4·7-litre	Ronnie Bucknum/Hans Müller
R. R. C. Walker (prepared by Shelby American)	4·7-litre	Bob Bondurant/Umberto Maglioli
Ford Advanced Vehicles	4·7-litre	John Whitmore/Innes Ireland
Ford-France	4·7-litre	Maurice Trintignant/Guy Ligier

It was interesting to see the Scuderia Filipinetti batting for both sides, and the Rob Walker entry was a car loaned to run in his name because the Serenissima (née ATS) coupés he was due to enter failed to materialise. The Ford-France car was an open model. Ford had now abandoned all pretence of running in National colours and the cars were in different bright colours for identification purposes. Whereas, under the *aegis* of Broadley and Wyer, the Ford Equipe at Le Mans the previous year had been compact and efficient, it now seemed that all 50 of the staff of the Ford Special Vehicles Department were at Le Mans besides the Shelby and Slough staff. Certainly, there were too many staff, not really knowing what each other was doing and generally getting in each others' way.

Of the Ford drivers, the oldest was Ken Miles, who was 46. He was a native of Sutton Coldfield, and before emigrating to America in 1952 had raced motor cycles and a Frazer Nash. In the States he had built up an excellent reputation as a driver of his own MG special, Porsche and Ferrari cars, but he did not achieve real prominence until he joined the Cobra project as chief test driver in 1963 and the following year he became Shelby's Competition Adviser. He played an important part in Shelby's development programme for the Ford and did most of the test driving in the States of the Mk II. Apart from his obsession with motor racing, Miles placed tremendous importance on keeping fit, and despite his age went for a run every day before breakfast.

Umberto Maglioli was another of the elders of motor racing, for he had been a member of the works Ferrari team in 1953 and 1954. He had driven the brutish 4·9-litre Ferrari in both the 1954 Mille Miglia and Le Mans races, and as late as 1964 was seen at the wheel of a works Ferrari. Another Ford driver of especial interest was Ronnie Bucknum, a 29-year-old Californian. As an amateur driver in the States he had achieved a great deal of success and was four

Above: The 7-litre Mk II of Bucknum and Hutcherson which finished third in the 1966 Le Mans race. *Below:* The 4-litre P3 which Mike Parkes and Lodovico Scarfiotti drove in the 1966 race, but it was eliminated by a collision with a CD at the Esses

The finish at Le Mans, 1966 – the official winner Bruce McLaren (who co-drove with Chris Amon) and Ken Miles (co-driver Denis Hulme) lead Ron Bucknum (co-driver Dick Hutcherson) across the line

times West Coast Champion in the Sports Car Club of America competition. He was obviously a competent and experienced driver, but not in World Championship class, and did not achieve prominence internationally until selected by Honda to drive their Grand Prix Car in its first experimental season.

It was evident that no one else was going to get a look in with the tremendous battle between the Fords and the Ferraris dominating the race, but there were other entries of interest. In addition to two 8-cylinder Porsche coupés and a 6-cylinder model, the Owen Organisation had entered the gas-turbine Rover-BRM. In the hands of Graham Hill and Jackie Stewart this was going to whistle its way round the Sarthe circuit for 24 hours without worrying anyone (though it did have fuel consumption problems), and it produced some consolation for those enthusiasts who would have liked to see the British car battling for the lead.

There was a new Maserati driven by Siffert and Neerpasch, and although it was good to see a new competition car from the Modena concern, it symbolised a tragedy. At the 1965 Le Mans test day, the car entered for the previous year's race by Maserati France had crashed with fatal results for its driver, American Lloyd Casner. Casner had formed the 'Camoradi Team' of sports/racing Maseratis which had raced during the years 1960–62, and in a sense the new car, the Tipo 65, was a tribute to his memory. Colonel Simone, head of Maserati France, was the last of the private owners to race Maseratis and did not want the name to disappear completely from the circuits. The Tipo 65, designed by Guilio Alfieri at Modena, had been built in France and work had not started until the beginning of May. It featured a V-8 Maserati engine bored out to 5044 cc and developing 430 bhp at 6500 rpm, mounted at the rear of a chassis constructed from a multitude of small-section tubes and with a very aerodynamic open body. In practice it showed a good turn of speed, but appeared to be difficult to handle on the straights. It ran off the road on the first lap of the race when in fourth position, damaging the radiator, and retired two laps later. Another interesting entry was the V-8 Chevrolet Iso Grifo with independent rear suspension and a fibreglass body. The Grifo was the competition version of the Iso Rivolta, and both were the work of Giotto Bizzarini. Bizzarini, a former Ferrari employee, was also responsible for the general layout of the Lamborghini. This very beautiful front-engined coupé was not really a pure competition car, but a 'hot' version of a touring model. It was driven by de Mortemart and Fraissinet, who had run a Cobra in the 1964 race, and lapped consistently to finish ninth.

For the first time in the history of the race the first practice session had to be cancelled. A torrential rainstorm inundated the course and winds of gale force blew trees down around Le Mans. Joakim Bonnier, for the Grand Prix Drivers' Association, did a couple of exploratory laps with the Maranello 365/P and on his advice the Automobile Club de l'Ouest abandoned practice. At the first practice session to be held Ford spent the time sorting out the cars and they did not settle down to serious lapping until the extra session added on the Friday evening. Surtees on Thursday had set an unofficial new lap record of 3 min 38·1 sec, but this was completely shattered on Friday by Phil Hill with the 7-litre Ford who turned in a lap of 3 min 33 sec (141·5 mph) – a time which showed how accurate Roy Lunn's predicted lap speeds for the 7-litre had been.

After all the publicity given to the Ford project, both to its failures in 1964 and its more successful outings in 1965, Ford felt that they had to win if there was not to be a severe loss of prestige to the Dearborn Company. In the Ford headquarters there reigned a rather noisy confidence, and remarks such as: 'Boy, we're gonna blow them red cars right off the track' were frequently to be heard. One man more than any other had been encouraged by the Ford fastest lap – the driver himself, Phil Hill, who was quietly hoping that the 7-litre would hold together and that at long last there would be a break in his run of bad luck. Since his win in the 1961 Drivers' Championship, he had enjoyed little success. The 1962 season had seen his Ferrari outclassed, 1963 was his year of failure with the ATS and in 1964 as second-string in the Cooper team he had generally driven a sub-standard car. Constant failure, even though it be the car's fault and not his own, weakens a driver's confidence in himself, and the situation can reach the stage where the driver is no longer sure whether he is imagining shortcomings in the handling or power output of his car or whether he is subconsciously inventing them to excuse his own poor performances.

Weather conditions were perfect at the start on Saturday afternoon with a clear sky and warm sunshine. After withdrawals, the number of starters had been reduced to 51. While the spectators sunbathed, Chris Amon shot into the lead with fellow New Zealander McLaren tucked in behind. At the end of the first lap the leaders had swapped positions and Surtees' Ferrari, which had got away in 15th spot, had climbed through the field to third. The battle of the giants was on, and was to continue unabated until the ranks of both Dearborn and Maranello were decimated. By lap 3 Baghetti had abandoned the Dino at the pits with engine trouble and a spin had dropped Surtees to fifth place. Trintignant brought the open Ford into the pits with a misfire.

McLaren in the lead twice broke the lap record, but the honour passed to Amon on lap 5 with a time of 3 min 37·7 sec (138·32 mph). Bondurant passed Guichet to take third place, but already Surtees was in the picture again and was close up behind Guichet, keeping a watching brief. Only a little over an hour had elapsed when McLaren and Amon came in to refuel, and they restarted in seventh and ninth places respectively. Although neither of the leading Fords was travelling along the Mulsanne Straight as fast as Hill had in practice (he had allegedly attained 213 mph) McLaren was officially timed at 199 mph. By 6 pm the McLaren/Miles Ford had re-asserted itself at the front and held a 22-second lead over the Surtees/Scarfiotti Ferrari with the Maranello Concessionaires car of Bonnier and Piper third.

It already appeared that Ford's challenge was weakening, for the Phil Hill/Chris Amon car had never managed to move up to the front again after its first fuel stop and the Shelby pit was desperately anxious about the state of the transmission. Bob Bondurant retired the Ford entered in Rob Walker's name with a blown cylinder head gasket, then the Filipinetti GT40 pulled in with gearbox trouble and the Hill/Amon car came in for the gear selector mechanism to be sorted out. An hour later, the situation was truly desperate for Ford, as Ferraris were in the first five places. The Miles/McLaren 7-litre had fallen back to sixth position, also suffering with gearbox trouble, and not long afterwards this caused its retirement. At nine, Whitmore took over from Ireland the Ford Advanced Vehicles entry sponsored by the *Weekend Telegraph*, found that it was over heating and returned to the pit. Ireland went out with the car again and two laps later returned it stinking of hot metal and with the exhausts glowing red. Of the entire Ford challenge, there was now only one car left, the 7-litre of Hill and Amon, well down the field after a lot of work on the gearbox. Although it was lapping very fast, it seemed inevitable, and this was confirmed by the expressions on the faces of the Shelby pit staff, that the gearbox would not last long. By 11 pm the last of the Fords was out of the race.

With the disappearance of the Ford opposition, the race lost much of its interest. The roads out of the circuit were jammed with departing spectators, the sideshows became even more crowded and the campers began to settle down for the night. Parked behind the Press stand was a Peugeot 404, doors locked, engine running. An hour later it was still there, bonnet red hot and a puzzled gendarme undecided what to do.

While the Ferraris had been lapping steadily and fast, the Ford opposition had gently crumbled away, but now Ferrari's troubles started. Surtees brought in the leading car with collapsed front suspension and a long time was lost changing the coil spring unit. Both the Maranello Concessionaires cars were in trouble, the 4·4-litre with a broken exhaust manifold and the 275LM with a broken gearbox. All the prototype Ferraris except the 275LMs were having brake trouble caused by the use of a new type of disc with radial ventilation. As these cars stopped altogether or wasted a lot of time sorting out their troubles, so the slower, but more reliable 275LMs came to the fore. At 4 am on Sunday morning the Dumay/Gosselin car had a two-lap lead over the similar car of Rindt and Gregory and the 275GTB of Mairesse and 'Beurlys' was lying third. All three works Ferraris were back in the race, using a mixture of solid and perforated discs, but they were so far back that they were not in the running.

The Ferrari mechanics had had a night of non-stop work on the various Maranello cars, and just when they were hoping for a cup of coffee and a break, Surtees reappeared in the pit with the 4-litre. A gearbox bearing had broken up and leaked oil on to the external clutch at the back of the gearbox. During another long pit stop the clutch was replaced, but Surtees only covered a couple of laps before a gearbox shaft broke. No sooner had the mechanics finished with the works car, than the NART 365/P came in with the same trouble. This was cured and the car finished to take seventh place and win its class. In the meanwhile the Bandini/Biscaldi 275/P had gone out with engine trouble and the remaining 4-litre car of Parkes and Guichet had both a weakening gearbox and an internal water leak. It continued to stagger round at reduced speed until 3 pm when it finally succumbed.

Interest was now focussed on the two leading 275LMs. The yellow Belgian-entered car was gradually being caught by the NART entry and their positions were finally reversed when Dumay suffered a burst tyre on the Mulsanne Straight. He limped back to the pits on the rim with the wheel sadly buckled and the bodywork crumpled. The bodywork was bashed clear with a spade, a new wheel fitted and the car rejoined the race with all hopes of victory dashed, for the NART car of Gregory and Rindt now had a five-lap lead. At 4 pm the first car to receive the chequered flag was the battered Belgian car, which was still five laps in arrears. In all there were only 14 finishers, and the winning NART entry was the first privately-owned Ferrari to win the race since Luigi Chinetti's victory in 1949.

RESULTS

1st	M. Gregory/J. Rindt (Ferrari 275LM) (Distance covered 2906·23 miles at 121·09 mph)
2nd	P. Dumay/G. Gosselin (Ferrari 275LM)
3rd	W. Mairesse/'Beurlys' (Ferrari 275GTB)
4th	H. Linge/P. Nocker (Porsche 8-cylinder)
5th	G. Koch/A. Fischhaber (Porsche 904GTS)
6th	A. Boller/D. Spoerry (Ferrari 275LM)
7th	P. Rodriguez/N. Vaccarella (Ferrari 365/P)
8th	J. Sears/R. Thompson (Shelby Cobra Daytona)
9th	J. de Mortemart/J. Fraissinet (Iso Grifo)
10th	G. Hill/J. Stewart (Rover-BRM)
11th	P. Hopkirk/A. Hedges (MGB)
12th	P. Hawkins/J. Rhodes (Austin Healey Sprite)
13th	J. Thuner/S. Lampinen (Triumph Spitfire)
14th	J. Piot/C. Dubois (Triumph Spitfire)

The winner of the Index of Performance was the Linge/Nocker Porsche.

For Ford, Le Mans had been an exciting and dramatic failure. Although they had again not won, their 7-litre cars were clearly faster than the Ferraris, and they now had to find the reliability to match their performance. Although in Shelby's hands the cars had shown tremendous potential, the efforts during the season of the Ford Advanced Vehicles of Slough had been rather pathetic and half-hearted; this was partly because they were concentrating on preparing for production the GT40, which came out later in the year. Ford had been worried about the effects of failing at Le Mans, and the bad publicity that would ensue. Generally, however, they received a reasonable press, for the works Ferraris had performed little better and the Ford image remained largely untarnished.

There remained one further race to end off the season, the Rheims

12-hours in July, but neither Ford nor Ferrari entered. Altogether there were only 22 starters and 13 finishers, and victory went to the NART 365/P of Rodriguez and Guichet with the similar Maranello Concessionaires entry, driven by Surtees and Parkes, in second place.

When he was not driving for Ferrari, or one of the private teams, John Surtees drove one of Eric Broadley's latest Lola T70 sports cars powered by the American Chevrolet V-8 engine. Cars such as these and the Oldsmobile-engined McLaren and Ford-engined Lotus 40 were not Grand Touring prototypes but virtually two-seater racing cars and loosely classified as 'sports cars'. There were no events for these cars on the European Continent, but they were widely raced in Great Britain and the United States. In 1965 they became recognised by the FIA as Group 9, later revised to Group 7. At the end of the European season most of the leading drivers competed with these cars in the 'Can-Am' series of races in the United States and Canada. It was driving in one of these events that John Surtees was seriously injured when the Lola lost a wheel. For a while, it seemed that he would never race again.

EIGHT
1966

From Prototype to Production

For the 1966 season an important change made by the Federation Internationale de l'Automobile was to reduce the number of cars needed to be built to qualify as a Grand Touring car from 100 to 50, these now being known as Competition GT cars. These formed Group 4, whereas Group 6 was the category for Prototype and Sports Cars, of which only one need have been built. Sufficient of Ferrari's 275LMs had now been built to qualify for Group 4 and Ford provided their answer with a production version of the GT40, of which the necessary 50 had been built at Slough in late 1965. The only major difference between the production version and the earlier prototypes was the adoption of a ZF 5-speed gearbox. The production GT40 was priced at £5500 (plus £1148 Purchase Tax), compared with the basic United Kingdom price for the 275LM of £9450. Although available rather more starkly fitted for competition use, road-going versions of the GT40 had a very luxurious trim and all the usual things such as map pockets, ashtrays and a cigarette lighter. Choice of gear ratios, axle ratios and colour finish were left to the customer, but the interior was trimmed in black. If possible, John Wyer liked the buyer to go to Slough for a personal fitting for his car, and likened its purchase to buying an exclusive Savile Row suit. De-tuned for road use, power output was 335 bhp at 6250 rpm and Wyer claimed the following performance in the gears:

     1st 58 mph
     2nd 90 mph
     3rd 127 mph
     4th 142 mph
     Top 164 mph

Among the first buyers were the American Essex Wire Corporation who planned to run a team of these cars in the 1966 Grand Touring

Championship. Carroll Shelby no longer contested this himself, as the production Ford rendered the Cobra obsolete, but he was now also involved in Dan Gurney's Eagle Grand Prix project run by All American Racers Inc., in addition to his Ford commitments, so he remained very fully occupied.

Revisions to the Mk II

Despite the failures of the 7-litre cars at Le Mans, Ford were well satisfied with the basic concept and felt that they had primarily let themselves down by racing the cars with insufficient testing. The Mk II had achieved all that was expected of it as far as lap times were concerned, and even if Fords had raced only 4·7-litre cars they would not have won, as the original model was simply not as fast as the Ferraris in 1965. To avoid repeating the mistakes of 1965 Lunn initiated a concentrated development programme falling into two categories. There was extensive testing at Daytona, Sebring and Riverside tracks with Ken Miles doing most of the driving, and specialised development programmes on different components. Development was speeded up by use of a special dynamometer evolved by Ford engineers. With this it was possible to run the engine and transmission units under simulated road conditions, these conditions having previously been recorded on tape in a vehicle fitted with recording instruments. In this way, component testing could continue regardless of whether a car was available when the engineers wanted it, and regardless of weather conditions.

It was concluded that no major changes were needed to either the engine or to the transmission unit of the Mk II cars. After the Le Mans cars had been stripped down it was found in one case that a speck of sand in the clutch slave cylinder had caused the piston to stick and generate heat at the throw-out bearing. The heat generated had softened an oil retaining ring in the axle and this had caused a loss of oil. On the other car a gear had broken because it had not been properly drilled. Both these points were easily dealt with.

There were, however, detail changes to be made to the chassis and body. A new, shorter nose was fitted to save weight and improve the aerodynamics. More efficient radiators were used, external rear brake scoops were added and there was improved ducting to the radiators, carburettors and brakes. Ventilated disc brakes were used, and because Ford were unable to solve completely the problem of brake discs cracking they decided to use a type of brake disc that could be changed almost as quickly as the pads.

The J-Car

In addition to the production GT40 and Mk II developments, Ford had evolved a third line of attack, known as the 'J-car' because it complied with Appendix J of the Group 6 regulations. Work started on this car in September, 1965, and the idea behind it was to use the lightest and strongest structural technique possible. While Lunn and his colleagues worked on the project at Kar-Kraft, others at Ford's Corporate Projects Studio worked out an advanced aerodynamic body shape.

The suspension design of the 'J' followed the Mk II, but it was the body/chassis structure which was completely new. This consisted of an aluminium honeycomb material sandwiched between two thin sheets of aluminium bonded together with an immensely powerful epoxy resin and riveted in areas where the stress was high. Suspension pick-up points and similar components were in steel or aluminium, and these too were bonded to the main structure. Although the engine was the usual 7-litre unit fitted to the Mk II, the 'J' had the exhausts grouped in fours on each side of the engine and running into their own tail pipes instead of the 'cross-over' system of the Mk II. Following Chaparral's lead in this field, the 'J' used automatic transmission. This was a Ford 2-speed and torque-converter transmission of the fully hydraulic type. The 'gear leaver' operated a valve that permitted the hydraulic mechanism to select 'drive', 'low' or 'high'.

In appearance the 'J' was graceful and dramatic without lumps, bumps and unnecessary projections. From the low-level air-intake with built-in spoilers close to the ground on either side, the body smoothly curved over the wheels, broken only by the flush perspex covers over the four headlights and a radiator extractor in front of the windscreen, to the roof-line, which ran straight back to the chopped tail in a manner reminiscent of the original Lola-Ford. Because of this roof-line it was necessary to use a rear-view mirror mounted on the roof and the driver looked at it through a slot in the roof.

The 'J' was tested at the Ford Proving Ground in March and then was shipped straight to Le Mans for the test week-end at the beginning of April. Here it ran with a recorder in the passenger seat which was instrumented to measure such matters as engine rpm, throttle openings, suspension movements and brake temperatures. Although the 'J' lapped Le Mans almost as fast as the modified Mk II-As which were doing a little over 140 mph, it was obviously far from raceworthy, and there was even talk of the honeycomb structure starting to melt.

A new Contender from the States

Following his success at Sebring in 1965, Jim Hall of the Chaparral team decided to build a car to comply with the Group 6 Regulations. Chaparrals are made in a small works near the town of Midland in Texas, most of the design work is done by Jim Hall himself and Hap Sharp, who drove with him in the Sebring race. The name Chaparral comes from that of a Texas desert bird which can run but not fly.

The first Chaparral was a front-engined car built for Hall by the Trautmann and Barnes speed shop in California in 1961, but the first to be built in his own works was a rear-engined car constructed by Sharp and their two mechanics during the winter of 1962 and early 1963 while Hall was in Europe driving a Grand Prix Lotus for Ken Gregory's British Racing Partnership Team. Hall never made much of a mark as a Grand Prix driver, but he gained a great deal of very useful experience. The 1963 car, known as the Chaparral 2, had a monocoque fibreglass chassis and a 5·3-litre V-8 Chevrolet engine. From this was developed the first Chaparral to have the 2-speed automatic transmission, and a later car had an aluminium chassis.

Hall's car for the 1966 season was known as the 2D. It had reverted to a fibreglass chassis, for Hall felt that the durability and non-fatiguing properties of the material justified the greater weight compared with sheet aluminium. Suspension was by double wishbones and coil springs at the front and rear. The power unit was a 5360 cc (102 × 83 mm) V-8 Chevrolet developed from that used in the Corvette 'Gran Sport' and fitted with downdraught Weber carburettors and separate exhaust systems for each bank of cylinders. An unusual feature of the Chaparral were the wheels, which were on the split-rim principle. The wheel was in two parts, held together by a ring of eight bolts. A magnesium alloy casting formed an integral hub and inner part of the rim joined by complex webbing. The tyre and tube were slid over the wheel and the outer part of the wheel was then pushed in place and the eight bolts fitted through the joining rib. According to the tyre section being used, alternative outer portions could be used to give different rim widths. The body was a neat fixed-head coupé with gull-wing doors and looking very much like the General Motors 'Mako Shark' dream car. On the roof there was a large scoop to deflect air down onto the carburettor, and the tail of the body turned up to meet with an adjustable spoiler – the preceding model had had a spoiler that was fully adjustable from the cockpit, but this had been abandoned on the 2D.

The most striking feature of the Chaparral team was their quiet and modest approach to racing. They toured Europe with an inconspicuous Chevrolet pick-up truck and closed trailer – a pleasant change from the overpoweringly wealthy display of equipment of the Ford organisation. In 1966 the team drivers for the Chaparral were Phil Hill and Joakim Bonnier. Depite this entry into top-level International racing, General Motors kept very much out of the picture, and the attitude adopted by the team was that similarities between features of the Chaparral and things done by General Motors were a sheer coincidence.

Before the European Season

At the beginning of February was held the Daytona race, but it had now been extended to a full 24 hours, and it is likely that the organisers did this knowing that Ford wished to have a full 24-hour race test before Le Mans. Ferrari's attitude was one of rather phoney apathy. At the annual Ferrari reunion in late 1965 he had laid great emphasis on the vast sums Ford were spending in their efforts to win at Le Mans and went on to say: 'Poor little us – what can we do against the might of Detroit?' Which, all things considered, especially his financial backing from Fiat, was something of a distortion of the true situation. Ferrari did not enter at Daytona, and sent only one car to Sebring; at the last moment he backed out of running at the Le Mans Test Week-end. At this time there were even suggestions that Ferrari would not run in the Le Mans race itself just to ensure that Ford's victory would be a hollow one.

Ford, however, were at Daytona in strength, and to back up the Shelby organisation, they had entered into racing contracts with both Alan Mann and the Holman and Moody organisation. John Holman was the engine specialist who had been responsible for the development work on the Ford saloons which had enjoyed a good run of success in American stock-car (production saloon) events. Thirty-two-year-old Mann, who enjoyed his hunting, shooting and fishing as much as he did his motor racing activities, had first come to the fore with the preparation of Ford Cortina saloons for the British Ford rally team. In 1965 he had been responsible for the preparation of the works Shelby Cobras at several important European meetings. Daytona was dominated by Fords, but they had nothing in the way of opposition. The Shelby entries of Ken Miles/Lloyd Ruby and Dan Gurney/Jerry Grant led home the Holman and Moody car of Walt Hansgen and Mark Donohue. Nevertheless, the winning Ford had pushed up the race average speed by nearly 10 mph, which in itself was quite an achievement (remembering that the race now lasted twice as long). The NART 365/P Ferrari of Rodriguez and Andretti finished fourth.

Six weeks later a solitary works Ferrari, together with a NART entry, did battle with an assortment of six Ford Prototypes and two Chaparrals at Sebring. That Ferrari was not matching Ford's pace of development could be seen by comparing the latest cars from the two teams. Ferrari's car, now known as the 330/P3, was almost identical to the previous year's 330/P2 mechanically, but had a new and more aerodynamic body of fibreglass. Mechanical changes were the use of Lucas fuel injection instead of Weber carburettors and Girling ventilated disc brakes, an attempt to banish the brake troubles that had afflicted the cars at Le Mans the previous year.

At Sebring the car was driven by Mike Parkes and Bob Bondurant, while the NART entry was handled by Pedro Rodriguez, the young Mexican driver and Mario Andretti. Andretti, who was 26 years old and came from Nazareth, Pennsylvania, was only 5 ft 5 in. tall. He was a vastly experienced driver in American stock car and Indianapolis-type events, but a newcomer to European-style racing. The NART car was one of the previous year's P2s fitted with the latest type of body.

In opposition were a horde of Fords, six prototypes, backed up by a total of 11 production GT40s, which included the very fast cars of the Essex Wire Corporation. Heading the Ford onslaught was the 7-litre car of Ken Miles and Lloyd Ruby – an open version of the Mk II known as the X-1 and declared by the drivers to be even hotter in the cockpit than the coupés – and a Mk II coupé for Dan Gurney and Jerry Grant, both entered by Carroll Shelby. The open car had first appeared at the Canadian Sports Car Grand Prix at Mosport in 1965 and in the first practice session at Sebring had automatic transmission but this gave trouble and was removed. Holman and Moody fielded an ordinary Mk II for Walt Hansgen and Mark Donohue, while another experimental car entered by this team was a Mk II with 2-speed automatic transmission and driven by A. J. Foyt and Ron Bucknum. Alan Mann Racing had two 4·7-litre GT40s for Graham Hill and Jackie Stewart, Sir John Whitmore and Frank Gardner. These had an aluminium body shell which reduced weight by about 120 lb. and because of this they were in the prototype class.

Practice revealed that although Ferrari's attitude about developing his prototypes meant that they were still no match for the Fords in terms of sheer speed, they were only marginally slower on the more difficult circuits with lap speeds below 110 mph. Gurney's sizzling 2 min 54·6 sec in practice was closely matched by Parkes with the Ferrari, which was but two seconds slower. The Chaparrals were showing themselves in practice to have an excessive thirst for oil that had Hall worried, and the fastest of the Chaparral drivers was Sharp, who managed 2 min 59·6 sec, sixth fastest. The works P3 had engine trouble in practice which necessitated changing the unit and the NART car with a time of 3 min 1·9 sec only was ninth fastest and slower than both the Chaparrals.

The race was ceremoniously started by Mr Haydon Burns, Governor of the State of Florida, who had not much idea of what he was doing and had to be given a firm nudge before he would drop the flag. First car away from the Le Mans start was the 2-litre Dino driven by Scarfiotti, and this led for half a lap before being overwhelmed by the heavy metal. Into the lead shot the Alan Mann Ford of Graham Hill with Parkes keeping the nose of the Ferrari right up the Ford's exhaust pipes. Gurney had had difficulty in inducing his Ford to start, and was frantically weaving his way through the field in an attempt to get to grips with the leaders.

Behind the two leaders were a whole pack of Fords, and mixed up with them the NART 330/P2, the Dino and the Chaparrals. Parkes took the lead and Rodriguez with the 330/P2 moved up into second place as the Fords ran into early troubles. Walt Hansgen pitted to have a loose door catch fixed, Hill came briefly into the pits for a plug change and Foyt brought the Holman and Moody car in with brake trouble which meant changing the front pads.

By lap 20, Parkes had a 20-second lead over the open Ford of Ken Miles, who in turn led Gurney. Dan Gurney had carved his way right through the field, setting in the process a new lap record of 2 min 54·8 sec (107·09 mph). He now took the open Ford and began to close up on Parkes. With a single car team entry, Parkes could not afford to become involved in a wild dice with the Fords; he let Gurney through into the lead and kept a watching brief behind him.

With two hours of the race over, both Chaparrals were out, with an insatiable thirst for oil and broken transmission respectively. The automatic Ford had an equally insatiable appetite for brake pads. Miles had difficulty in starting the open Ford after a pit stop, but even so had made up for lost time and passed the Ferrari to take second place. As his two entries diced with each other for the lead, Carroll Shelby became frantic in the Ford pit and furiously waved a hammer at Ken Miles in an attempt to induce him to ease off. Fourth was the Alan Mann car of Hill and Stewart, but it had a monumental spin with Stewart at the wheel and time had been wasted patching up the tattered fibreglass. By the half-way mark the Parkes/Bondurant Ferrari was back in second place and the NART car was holding on to fourth spot. Two hours later the positions were unchanged – and all three leading cars were on the same lap, with the NART car in fourth place but five laps in arrears. Throughout the race the automatic Ford was in and out of the pits for brake pad changes and the Holman and Moody mechanics had lost track of how many times they had changed them. The Alan Mann car of Whitmore and Gardner retired with clutch failure.

An hour later and the Ferrari challenge had faded. Bondurant was forced to stop out on the circuit with a seized gearbox and soon the NART car found itself in trouble. After a pit stop for work on the lights, Andretti selected first instead of second gear going into one of the corners; the Ferrari spun and collided with a Porsche which was thrust through the spectator barrier. Four spectators who had wandered to an unofficial vantage point were killed by the Porsche. Andretti limped back to the pits, unaware of the results of his spin and with the front of the Ferrari smashed in and only one headlamp working. The bodywork was sorted out and Andretti tried to restart the car, but without success. Fuel vapour poured from the exhausts, the pit marshal shouted a warning about the fuel gas and seized an extinguisher. Hearing the word fuel, one of the

Italian mechanics sloshed a bucket of water under the rear of the car. The bucket grazed the ground, sending up sparks, and in a moment the Ferrari was ablaze. Although the fire was soon extinguished, the Ferrari was out of the race. The Dino was limping round with partially collapsed suspension, but was still well placed.

As the finishing hour approached, it seemed that the Dan Gurney and Jerry Grant car must win, as it had gained a lap's lead over the open car, partly because the open car had been delayed by the replacement of a cracked disc. While the chequered flag was being held ready at the finish and the leading blue Ford was completing its lap, the engine spluttered and cut out. Gurney coasted as far as he could and then started to push the heavy car towards the finishing line – alas in vain, because the race stewards ruled that as the Regulations provided that cars must lap the circuit only under their own power, the Ford must be disqualified.

With Fords in the first three places and a Porsche fourth it was Ferrari's turn to learn a lesson. If the make's prestige was not to be damaged, especially in its most important market, he would have to make a more determined effort in American races. Not only were the Fords a match for Ferrari in terms of performance, but by sheer weight of numbers they could steamroller their way to victory against a solitary entry.

The Le Mans Test Week-end

At the last moment Ferrari sent a telegram to the Automobile Club de l'Ouest saying that his cars would not be attending the test week-end, because they had adequate facilities for testing at Monza. Although this appeared to be another phase in Ferrari's apathetic reaction to the Ford challenge it was, in fact, a very intelligent move. It meant that Fords had nothing against which to judge their lap times on the Sarthe circuit and no means of knowing what the works Ferraris would be capable of in June.

Ford turned up at the Le Mans test week-end in force with three Shelby Mk IIs in addition to the 'J' which has already been described. Alan Mann was also there with his two 4·7-litre cars distinguished by their colour finish of red with gold stripes and quick-action oil pipe connectors protruding from the offside of the bodywork through which oil could be injected straight into the sump during a pit stop. Without the Ferraris the test week-end lost much of its excitement and much of the time was spent on tyre tests with the products of Dunlop, Goodyear and Firestone. A dull occasion for the 30,000 spectators became a very unhappy one when veteran American driver Walt Hansgen lost control of one of the Mk IIs on the pit straight and crashed in the escape road. He suffered multiple injuries, and although flown to hospital by helicopter, died soon afterwards.

Monza 1000 Kilometres Race

Perhaps the most welcome sight at Monza in April was to see John Surtees back at the wheel of a Ferrari and almost fully recovered from his near-fatal accident in Canada the previous September. At Monza he led the Ferrari attack with Mike Parkes at the wheel of Ferrari's latest P3 models which had proper coupé bodywork. The other works Ferrari entries were two of the very pretty and potent 2-litre Dinos. The example driven by Bandini and Scarfiotti had closed bodywork and looked very much like the baby brother of the P3. Two other works-supported Dinos were entered by Maranello Concessionaires and the Scuderia St Ambroeus. The other works Dino was an open car, but Bondurant wrote this off during practice. This and the two privately-entered cars were on Weber carburettors, whereas the closed works Dino, like the P3, was on Lucas fuel injection and had twin ignition.

No 7-litre Fords were entered, as Shelby and the other official Ford teams were conserving their energies for Le Mans. Alan Mann had entered his GT40s, but they were withdrawn. The sight of privately-owned GT40s was already a common one, however, and at Monza there were the cars from the Essex Wire Corporation, F. English Ltd, Ford-France, Scuderia Filipinetti and the English private owner Nick Cussons. The F. English entry came from an English concern who are the main distributors for British Ford cars in Bournemouth. However, Colonel Ronnie Hoare of Maranello Concessionaires has a large stake in F. English so he, too, like the Scuderia Filipinetti, was batting for both teams.

The works P3 had the race sewn up from the start to the chequered flag; it rained during the race and although the Ferrari's wipers failed, its shape was such that most of the water swept over the roof and the car was not slowed. Wiper trouble, oddly enough, affected

At the Le Mans trials in 1966 Ford introduced the 'J' with a honeycomb aluminium sub-structure, but the car was not raced.

For 1967 Ford produced the Mk IV which incorporated a number of lessons learned in the development of the 'J' cars. On April 1st one of these cars scored a win in the Sebring 12-hours race. The drivers were Lloyd Ruby and A. J. Foyt – but once again no works Ferraris were entered

Above: The Chaparral has been faster on most circuits than either the Fords or Ferraris, but the cars are still plagued by mechanical unreliability and their chances are weakened by their never entering more than two cars. Phil Hill is seen during the 1966 Le Mans event. *Below:* The 1967 Chaparral was a much improved and redesigned car, distinguished by its stabilising wing

all the Dinos as well, and their mechanical trouble meant that the expected dice with the Porsche Carrera 6 entries did not materialise – the highest placed Dino, that of Bandini and Scarfiotti, was tenth. Surtees was able to do his full share of the driving with Parkes, and as the leading Ferrari had no opposition, it gave him an easier return to racing than could have been the case. At the finish he was very happy and relieved and had demonstrated that none of the old Surtees sparkle had been lost. The Essex Wire car of Gregory and Whitmore took second place from the similar Scuderia Filipinetti entry which was driven by Müller and Willy Mairesse.

The Targa Florio

As neither any Fords, apart from a Ford-France GT40 of Ligier and Greder, nor the Chaparral appeared, the battle of the Sicilian mountains became once again a straight duel between Ferrari and Porsche. And once again Ferrari pinned his hopes on a single large car and the Dinos. An open P3 was driven by local boy Nino Vaccarella and Lorenzo Bandini and as this pair had won the previous year they had great hopes of repeating their victory. The two works Dino Tipo 206s were driven by the pairs Mike Parkes and Lodovico Scarfiotti, and Jean Guichet and Giancarlo Baghetti, of which the first pair had an open car with fuel injection and the second pair a coupé. A Dino was again loaned to the Scuderia St Ambroeus.

Facing Ferrari was an immensely strong team of Porsches. All three had the long-snout 'Carrera' body and chassis with a long, slanted, tinted back window louvred where it passed over the engine and the same as Porsche, with their teutonic efficiency, had turned out at Stuttgart in sufficient numbers to comply with the Grand Touring regulations. One of these with an 8-cylinder engine enlarged to 2·2-litres was running in the Prototype category, while the other two were running as GT cars. Backing them up were a total of five Carrera 6 cars entered by private owners, but that of the Aldington brothers who used to build Frazer Nash cars and nowadays run Porsche Cars of Great Britain had been transferred to the prototype category. This was because the organisers were insisting that all Group 4 (i.e. 50 made) cars should have number plates and a log book and the British cars had neither. This car was driven by Mike de Udy and the young South African Peter de Klerk. So for once

Porsche had almost as many supporting cars in the race as did Ferrari, whose private ranks included three 275LMs.

During the week before the race some belated attempts were made to improve the surface, but the tarmac-laying efforts were frustrated by both the hot sun and a lot of unofficial lappery by people trying to learn the course. As 1966 was the fiftieth anniversary of the race there was held a commemorative run round the 148-kilometre Large Circuit of the Madonie, the mountain lap used for the early years of the race, for cars of the type that used to take part. Once this was over, the teams settled down to the major work of the day, official practice. This soon had Ferrari team manager Dragoni in a state of nerves, as it was found that the 2·2-litre Porsche was lapping faster than the P3, and his consternation increased when he learned that Mike Parkes had wrapped the Dino round a tree. Parkes was unhurt, and when the car was inspected, it was found that the damage was not as bad as had been expected, as it was limited to the front suspension and body. Even so, it meant more work for the Ferrari mechanics.

After a week of hot sunshine, torrential rain inundated the circuit from midday Saturday until midnight. This made a dreadful mess of the circuit with stones and mud everywhere, and a lot of hard work with brooms and shovels by hastily rounded-up gangs of workmen was needed to have the circuit ready for the start at 8 am. There was still a lot of mud about, however, and this made the going very difficult for the big Ferrari. At the end of the first lap it had a slight lead on time from Mitter with the 2-litre Porsche, but the Porsche forged ahead on the next lap. Soon Scarfiotti with the Dino was ahead of the P3, and the downfall of their hero made the locals very unhappy. To make matters worse for Ferrari, it had started to rain again. After the change of drivers, Bandini succeeded in holding the Porsche, now driven by Mitter and was second behind the 8-cylinder Porsche with Colin Davis at the wheel. Parkes had a leaking fuel tank and after re-fuelling he went away leaving a trail of petrol down the road. Not long afterwards he went off the road, wrecking the rear of the car. Bandini did not survive much longer either and was eliminated through an accident which was really no fault of his own. He was about to lap a 250GTO Ferrari when the driver signalled him to wait, but it was rather an ambiguous signal which Bandini misinterpreted as the more usual 'come on'. As he went past the two cars collided and the P3 left the road, rolled and was written off against a tree. The GTO driver then stopped and gave a cut and rather shaken Bandini a lift back to the pits.

The 8-cylinder Porsche had the left-hand rear suspension collapse and Mitter had left the road and bent the *front* suspension of his Porsche. All this excitement left the superbly driven and unscathed Porsche of Müller and Willy Mairesse firmly in the lead. It won at an average of 61·47 mph, which was slower than the previous year's speed, but not surprisingly so in view of the difficult conditions. The winning car was entered by the Scuderia Filipinetti (batting for *three* sides?), but the Porsche works had a hand in the victory as the car was loaned by them. In second place was the 2-litre Dino of Baghetti and Guichet. It was good to see Baghetti doing well, for he had never had much luck since the 1961 season, when hailed as the newly-discovered wonder boy of motor racing, he had won the French Grand Prix after the retirement of the other three works Ferraris.

After the results were announced, the Ford-France team managed by John Wyer put in a protest at the exclusion from the results of their GT40. This had retired with a broken stub axle about eight miles from the finishing line. The team had a point, for the regulations stipulated that any car covering not less than nine-tenths of the winner's distance would be classified in the results. Although it did not finish, the organisers were forced to give it 12th place, which meant a victory in the over 2000 cc sports class that would otherwise have gone to a 275LM

The Spa 1000 Kilometres Race

Although this was another race counting towards the Championship, Ford did not bother with the Spa race, and the only official entry was a 7-litre from Alan Mann driven by John Whitmore and Frank Gardner. There was, of course, the usual array of GT40s, and it was certain that one of these would have sewn up the Grand Touring Category for they were very much faster than the 275LMs. As was equally usual, Ferrari sent only one large prototype, a P3 for Mike Parkes and Lodovico Scarfiotti, backed up by a Dino loaned to Maranello Concessionaires and the privately-owned re-bodied P2s of Ecurie Francorchamps who were expected to do well on their home circuit, and David Piper whose co-driver was Mike Salmon.

The works P3 had the legs of the Alan Mann Ford in practice and simply ran away with the race. Not only was it faster than the Ford, but its Firestones were wearing well, whereas the Ford was getting through an awful lot of Goodyears. The works Porsches were simply outclassed in terms of speed and lacked their usual reliability mainly because they were overdriven, and on this fast circuit there were plenty of opportunities for over-revving – one of the works cars blew up because it had been taken over a thousand rpm above the limit. With 12 laps to go the P3 had a lead of nearly four minutes. While the Ferrari mechanics lolled against the pit with a quiet air of confidence Mike Parkes was jumping up and down trying to persuade Scarfiotti to ease off the pace, but he need not have worried; the P3 had not missed and did not miss a beat, and won convincingly. Third and fourth were the Essex Wire GT40 of Skip Scott and Peter Revson, and Peter Sutcliffe's own car which he shared with Brian Redman.

The Nürburgring 1000 Kilometres Race

At long last the Chaparral made its European debut with Phil Hill and Joakim Bonnier at the wheel. The drivers, well aware of what happens in the way of suspension troubles when a car runs at the Nürburgring for the first time, had tried to persuade Jim Hall to take the car to the circuit for a full week's testing before the race. Hall had refused, saying that everything had been worked out back home, and the car would be all right. Hill and Bonnier did not believe him and resigned themselves to trouble, but events were to prove them wrong. Ferrari again made only one entry in the large prototype class and although his drivers, Surtees and Parkes, used open and closed cars respectively in practice, they chose the coupé for the race. There were no works Fords in the race, but just the usual hordes of 4·7 GT40s. Porsche as usual were out in force on their home ground and fielded a total of five cars ranging from the 2·2-litre 8-cylinder car to a standard Carrera 6. Although there was a possibility of the 2·2-litre scoring an outright victory, team manager Hushke von Hanstein's main concern was victory in the 2-litre class, which meant warding off the three Dinos, one each entered by the works, Maranello Concessionaires and NART.

Fastest in practice was the works P3 with a time of 8 min 31·9 sec, but the Chaparral with Phil Hill at the wheel was less than four seconds slower, which was fantastic for a car on its first appearance at the Nurbürgring, and it was clear that Hill was not trying all that hard. Third fastest was the 8-cylinder Porsche, which lapped in the hands of Jochen Rindt at 8 min 44 sec.

With a circuit of 22·8 kilometres and around 350,000 spectators, the organising club like to have as many cars appearing as possible, to maintain the spectators' interest in the race, and 71 cars lined up for the Le Mans-type start. When the starting signal was given it was again a Dino that shot into the lead, the works fuel-injected car of Bandini. By the end of the first lap it was the P3 leading the Dino by 17 seconds with the Chaparral (Bonnier at the wheel) close behind and leading a tremendous and indistinguishable pack of Porsches, Dinos and GT40s. Two laps later and the P3 had a 50-second lead, and the Chaparral was past the Dino.

On lap 6 the one-car-domination-of-motor-racing-by-Ferrari-act went all wrong and the P3 staggered into the pits with collapsed rear suspension. After a pause while Chief Engineer Mauro Forghieri investigated, a mechanic was sent running for a replacement Koni damper/coil spring unit. The race was lost in the seven minutes needed to change the unit. The Chaparral led with Scarfiotti grimly hanging on behind it, just hoping that he would stay on the road. At quarter-distance (11 laps) the Chaparral came in to refuel and restarted with Hill at the wheel in third place, as the Porsches had already made their stops. Hill now really began to motor the Chaparral and by lap 16 was firmly back in the lead with a minute and a half in hand. Parkes was pushing the P3 up through the field and had climbed back to seventh place. On lap 17 Parkes stopped for fuel, Surtees took over again, but before he had completed a lap the eye-bolt of the damper unit again broke and he had to limp back to the pits. Surtees restarted with the car a lap behind the leading Chaparral and the second-place Dino. Ten laps later the P3 was back in the pits with clutch trouble, the mechanics adjusted this and Parkes took over, but it was not long before the P3s speed was reduced to a crawl again with clutch trouble, and it just made it back to the pits to retire.

With the race a little over three-quarters run, it started to rain. As soon as the road became wet the Chaparral, running on dry weather tyres, became almost uncontrollable and was sliding all over the track. Hill made it back to the pits, where there was a lengthy delay while a set of rain tyres with the tread specially cut by the Chaparral team themselves were fitted. By the time Hill had rejoined the race the rain had nearly stopped. He had a lead of only a minute, and it was anybody's guess how the car would handle on the rain tyres if the track dried out. In one lap, Hill added 24 seconds to his lead over the Dino and the track stayed wet, but he was not without his troubles. The wiper blades had slipped and disappeared under the scuttle, so Hill's vision was very limited, and while going though some of the slower bends he flipped open the gull-wing door and gave the outside of the screen a wipe. Hill crossed the finishing line nearly a minute ahead of the Dino in second place, and among the first to congratulate the Chaparral team were the Ferrari drivers Surtees and Parkes.

Le Mans

After the six 'warm-up' races of the 1966 season, that had preceded Le Mans, the score was three to Ferrari, two to Ford and one to Chaparral. The outcome of Le Mans was completely unpredictable, for the P3 and the Mk II had not yet met on truly equal terms. At Sebring the solitary Ferrari was a match for the Fords, but it had not Ferrari's fastest drivers. At Spa, a very fast circuit, the solitary Ford could have been expected to do well, but it was a rather tired car that had already campaigned at Daytona and Sebring. Furthermore in the 1966 race the 7-litre Fords had been faster than the Ferraris but since then Lucas fuel injection had given Ferrari a little extra bhp. One thing, however, was likely – the winner at Le Mans would not be the Chaparral. With a single-car entry again driven by Hill and Bonnier, there could be no question of sending out one car to break the opposition, and Chaparral's sole hope of victory was resting on the failure of the fastest cars of both Ford and Ferrari. This did not at all perturb Jim Hall, as he regarded 1966 as very much an exploratory season, and was more than satisfied with the victory at the Nurburgring – he reckoned on doing most of his winning during the 1967 season.

Although the Ford entry was divided up into three teams, with a total of eight 7-litre prototypes this force was united and co-ordinated, properly controlled from the pits and there would be no question of opposing teams driving each other into the ground. The Ford entry was made up as follows:

Drivers	Entrant
Ken Miles and Denis Hulme	Shelby American Inc.
Bruce McLaren and Chris Amon	Shelby American Inc.
Dan Gurney and Jerry Grant	Shelby American Inc.
Paul Hawkins and Mark Donohue	Holman and Moody Inc.
Ronnie Bucknum and Dick Hutcherson	Holman and Moody Inc.
Lucien Bianchi and Mario Andretti	Holman and Moody Inc.
Graham Hill and Brian Muir	Alan Mann Racing
John Whitmore and Frank Gardner	Alan Mann Racing

Supporting these were a total of five GT40s, two from the Essex Wire Corporation and one each from F. English Ltd, Scuderia Filipinetti and Ford-France. Ford had already had difficulty in scraping together 16 top-line drivers for their cars, not because no one wanted to drive for them as they did not pay enough (Fords pay their drivers about £500 for Le Mans, varying according to the individual) but because there are just not enough experienced and able drivers available. These difficulties were added to when American driver Dick Thompson had a collision during practice with Bob Holquist's GT40. The Grand Tourer left the road at Mulsanne and was wrecked. As far as everyone else was concerned, it was just one of those things that happen in motor racing, but the race officials alleged that Thompson had failed to report the accident in accordance with the Regulations and that Alan Mann was also at fault. Accordingly, they said, the car was disqualified from running. Fords' reaction was to announce the withdrawal of all their 7-litre cars. The officials of the Automobile Club de l'Ouest met to discuss the matter, but would not change their minds. Fords argued with them, admitting that a regulation had been contravened, but saying that the original ruling was grossly unfair. At last agreement was reached and face was saved for everyone except poor Dick Thompson! He was excluded from the race and Alan Mann was fined one dollar and given the chance to find another co-driver for Graham Hill. Brian Muir, the young Australian who raced a Galaxie and Cobras for John Willment, was flown over and given an observed practice session on the morning of the race. His driving satisfied the officials, but few other drivers have faced a race with such trepidation. Nevertheless, despite his unfamiliarity with the circuit and the car, his driving in the race was impeccable.

This incident, however, paled into insignificance alongside the row that had divided the Ferrari camp. Eugenio Dragoni, the Ferrari team manager, decided that Scarfiotti should be reserve driver for the works Ferraris and made it clear to John Surtees that he thought the former World Champion was still not fit enough to drive for more than a couple of hours. His idea was that Surtees should start the race, staying at the wheel for the first two hours or so, and that for the rest of the race the car would be driven by Parkes and Scarfiotti. Surtees bitterly resented this, as his drives at Monza in the 1000 kilometres race and at Spa in the Belgian Grand Prix, which he had won, more than amply demonstrated that he had regained his old form and fitness. Not only was this Dragoni making himself awkward once again, but it appeared that the direction had emanated from Enzo Ferrari himself and arose out of Surtees' inability for many laps to pass Jochen Rindt's Cooper-Maserati in the Belgian Grand Prix. At Spa the weather conditions had been dreadful, but once Surtees had passed the Cooper, he had forged ahead. Ferrari was not, of course, at Le Mans to speak for himself and Surtees felt that he had no alternative but to walk out on the team. He did this with very many regrets, as he was happy in the Ferrari Organisation, but there are limits to what a man can take. This was the eventual Ferrari line-up:

Drivers and car	Entrant
Mike Parkes and Lodovico Scarfiotti (P3)	Works
Lorenzo Bandini and Jean Guichet (P3)	Works
Pedro Rodriguez and Richie Ginther (P3)	North American Racing Team
Richard Attwood and David Piper (365/P2)	Maranello Concessionaires Ltd
'Beurlys' and Pierre Dumay (365/P2)	Ecurie Francorchamps
Masten Gregory and Bob Bondurant (365/P2)	North American Racing Team
Willy Mairesse and Hans Müller (365/P2)	Scuderia Filipinetti

Supporting the prototype Ferraris were three 275GTBs and a 275LM in the Grand Touring category and three Dinos which had a race of their own on with the Porsches and the Matras. Matra Sport were a division of the French aeronautical and space engineering concern, Engins Matra. When they started to take an interest in cars, they bought the René Bonnet concern who made Renault-

Above: Bearer of all British hopes in the 1967 race was the Lola Aston Martin. This is the car driven by Chris Irwin and Peter de Klerk. Both of them retired early in the race. *Below:* One of three Fords eliminated in the multi-car crash at Le Mans in 1967 was the Ford France-entered Mk II seen here about to be lapped by the second place Ferrari

Above: The second place Ferrari in the 1967 Le Mans race, driven by Mike Parkes and Ludovico Scarfiotti, sweeps down from the Dunlop Bridge to the Esses. *Below:* The product of JW Automotive Engineering is the Mirage, a modified version of the catalogued G.T.40 Mk III. The main external difference lies in the modified roof section, and one of these cars won the 1967 Spa 1,000-kilometre race

powered coupés on a small scale and were regular performers at Le Mans and elsewhere. Under the wing of Matra, the car side of the business moved into Formula 2 and 3 racing and for long distance prototype events had produced a fascinating BRM-powered coupé. The 2-litre Matra was of rather odd shape, but very efficient as it had been evolved in the company's aerodynamics department. The power unit was the 1½-litre V-8 BRM enlarged to 2 litres, fitted with Lucas fuel injection and developing something over 250 bhp. When the 2-litre Matras raced, they were attended by BRM mechanics. With three of these cars at Le Mans, three Dinos and a total of four Porsches, it looked as though competition in the 2-litre class would be very hot – especially as the Dino had beaten the Porsche at the Nurbürgring and Porsche were out to avenge that defeat!

Dan Gurney with his bright red Ford was fastest in practice with a fantastically fast time of 3 min 30·6 sec and he headed the long line-up of 55 starters. At the start Graham Hill with the silver Ford snatched the lead closely followed by Gurney. Ferraris were well up in the solid mass of Fords and held fifth, seventh and eleventh positions. There were no immediate changes and by 5 pm Ferraris had not strengthened their position. The highest placed Maranello car was Rodriguez in fourth spot with the NART P3. Already two of the Dinos had been eliminated by mechanical failures and the third did not last much longer. Already a lot of interest had gone out of the 2-litre class.

During the second hour it rained and when the leading Fords started to come in for fuel, they found their pits packed out with their less fortunate team-mates who were already in trouble. Among these was the car of Paul Hawkins and Mark Donohue which broke a drive-shaft on the Mulsanne straight causing the car to go broadside at nearly 200 mph. This had been replaced, but the car was in the pits again with rear axle trouble. When it rejoined the race, it ran into yet more trouble and lost its engine cowling which blew off along the Mulsanne straight. After the pattern of the race had settled down again with the fuel stops over the Gurney/Grant car led from that of Miles and Hulme. The highest placed Ferrari was the Rodriguez/ Ginther P3 sitting comfortably in third position.

Long before the fall of dark the hot pace of the race began to take its toll. To top all its earlier troubles the bronze-coloured car of Hawkins and Donohue went out with differential failure and Alan Mann's yellow car driven by Whitmore and Gardner was eliminated by clutch trouble. In addition all the Fords were suffering from excessive brake pad wear – it had been estimated that these pads would need changing every eight hours, but none were lasting longer than five. While at the front the Fords were leading the Ferraris, the Chaparral was running a steady 12th and at the tail of the field there were other excitements. The 6-cylinder 1300 cc ASA, based on a design for a baby Ferrari with which Enzo had toyed, collided on the Mulsanne straight with a Peugeot 204-engined CD and caught fire.

More troubles struck the Ford entries. The Hill/Muir car broke its suspension and the Bianchi/Andretti car broke its engine. The Chaparral retired quietly with electrical failure and the Ferrari of Scarfiotti and Parkes went out with a bang when Scarfiotti hit the other CD in the Esses. At midnight Ginther still held third place behind the two leading Fords, but midnight also marked the acme of the Ferrari endeavour and their forces began to wane. Ginther retired the NART car shortly afterwards with gearbox trouble and at 3.30 am, the most unpleasant time on that cold and damp night, the Filipinetti 4·4 retired for the same reason. As a misty dawn broke Ford held the first six places.

Many more retirements were to follow. The remaining works Ferrari, already well down at the tail of the field after a dose of assorted troubles and with no hope of victory, disappeared with overheating problems caused by an internal water leak. And the Gurney/Grant Ford, having set the pace for much of the race was out of water. There was no hope of it struggling on till it had covered sufficient laps to be allowed replenishment and Shelby reluctantly ordered its withdrawal.

By noon Fords held the first three positions followed by a phalanx of four Porsches. All six of the GT40s had retired, all three Matras had been eliminated, one by being unable to avoid Scarfiotti's crash. Heading the Grand Touring category was the Maranello Concessionaires' 275GTB with Formula 3 drivers Roy Pike and Piers Courage sharing the wheel. Shortly afterwards the GTB broke a brake pipe and Pike had to try and control his anxiety while he watched it being repaired and the system bled of air. The Ford pit was equally anxious for they thought, and with good reason, that any one, or all three, of their remaining cars could break. Rain started to fall at 2 pm and the remaining runners eased off so as to prevent anything silly happening to them with the race so nearly over. In the last half-hour the Fords bunched up together in a pre-arranged plan for McLaren and Miles to cross the line, headlamps ablaze, in a dead heat, with Bucknum as close behind as he could tuck himself. Equally impressive was the line of four Porsches occupying the next four places in general classification.

Unfortunately for Fords, the dead-heat that Henry Ford II had so proudly watched did not come off. The timekeepers decided to put a spoke in Fords' showmanship by announcing that a dead heat was impossible, as the cars had started at 4 pm on Saturday with the Miles/Hulme car already some yards ahead on the starting grid, with the result that, as they had arrived side-by-side at the finish 24 hours later, the McLaren/Amon car must have covered a greater distance, this being officially given as 20 metres.

RESULTS

 1st B. McLaren/C. Amon (Ford Mk II) – 126·01 mph
 2nd K. Miles/D. Hulme (Ford Mk II)
 3rd R. Bucknum/R. Hutcherson (Ford Mk II)
 4th C. Davis/J. Siffert (Porsche Carrera 6)
 5th H. Herrmann/H. Linge (Porsche Carrera 6)
 6th U. Schutz/P. de Kierk (Porsche Carrera 6)
 7th G. Klass/R. Stommelen (Porsche Carrera 6)
 8th R. Pike/P. Courage (Ferrari 275GTB)
 9th H. Grandsire/L. Cella (Alpine-Renault)
10th C. Dubois/P. Noblet (Ferrari 275GTB)
11th J. Cheinisse/R. de Lageneste (Alpine-Renault)
12th G. Verrier/R. Bouharde (Alpine-Renault)
13th M. Bianchi/J. Vinatier (Alpine-Renault)
14th 'Franc'/J. Kerguen (Porsche 911)
15th J. Marnat/C. Ballot-Leana (Mini-Marcos)

The Davis/Siffert Porsche won the Index of Performance
Fastest lap was by Dan Gurney in 3 min 30·6 sec (142.8 mph)

Three years and several million dollars after it all started, Ford had made the grade.

NINE
1967

Now that Ferrari was the Challenger

As well as being the most important race of the season, Le Mans was also the only race of the 1966 season in which Ferrari and Ford had met on truly equal terms. During 1966 the Fords had been faster in a straight line, generally more reliable and had better aerodynamics. Basically, however, the Ferrari was a more refined design technically. Ferrari did not intend matching Ford litre for litre and, as he had a fundamentally sound design, his obvious course was to improve it – but as the 1967 season progressed, it became clear that the improvements were insufficiently great. The main mechanical change, following the same lines of development as the Grand Prix cars, was the introduction of a 36-valve cylinder head, with two inlet and one exhaust valve per cylinder, which boosted power output to 450 bhp at 8000 rpm. To this engine was mated a new 5-speed Ferrari gearbox. Another change was the transfer of the brakes from the inboard position to the hubs, and this involved slight modifications to the rear suspension layout. The bodywork was lower and cleaner, and both open and coupé versions continued to be raced. The brakes were slightly larger and new and wider Campagnolo wheels were used.

While the works were racing the new model, known as the P4, Ferrari supplied his supporting private teams with a compromise model, not given any officially recognised title, but generally called the P3/4. These cars had a body like the P4, outboard rear brakes and the latest rear suspension changes, but with the 1966 engine running on Weber carburettors and a ZF 5-speed gearbox. One each of these went to the North American Racing Team (finished in red, blue and white), Maranello Concessionaires Ltd (red and pale blue), Équipe Nationale Belge (yellow) and Scuderia Filipinetti (red and white).

Strengthening of the Chaparral Challenge

Jim Hall had promised to campaign the 1967 European season of Prototype racing with a stronger team and he kept this promise in no uncertain terms with two vastly improved cars which had a novel technical feature in addition to the automatic transmission.

These were based on the Group 7 sports/racing cars which Hall had raced in the Can-Am series in the autumn of 1966 and had been designated by Hall as the 2E. They were open cars and were distinguished by an adjustable aerofoil or 'stabilising wing' mounted high above the rear wheels. The airflow on to this wing caused a downward pressure on to the rear wheels and improved adhesion on corners, while on the straights the wing could be set to a neutral position which improved the stability in a straight line. Operation of this wing was by a foot pedal in the cockpit. For the 1967 season Hall rebuilt these 2Es as coupés complying with the FIA Group 6 Prototype regulations. They became known as the type 2F and were powered by an even larger 7-litre Chevrolet-based engine, developing 525 bhp, which made them much more powerful than either of their immediate rivals. The Chaparral now had one-piece instead of split rim wheels. Another big advantage of the 2F was its low weight of 1800 lb. with fuel, but without driver, compared with 2600 lb for the 7-litre Ford in similar trim. To many eyes the 2F Chaparral was the ugliest car of its type racing, but the bodywork was superbly functional and decidedly reminiscent of the Ford 'J-car', a style of bodywork that Ford themselves abandoned for 1967.

For Daytona and Sebring at the beginning of the season Jim Hall had only one 2F ready and also raced the 1966 2D coupé in these races. In April both cars were ready and the modest Chaparral équipe transferred itself to European headquarters in Frankfurt, which Hall thought was central enough for getting to most of the European long-distance races and suited a number of the mechanics who were of German origin.

Dearborn Developments

As well as racing the existing Mk II 7-litre model, Lunn was busy at Kar-Kraft on a further development of the car which it was hoped would maintain Ford's superiority in the Prototype category. After the 1966 Le Mans practice day, work was shelved on the 'J' until

Fords had got the Le Mans race itself under their belts. Then at Kar-Kraft a new development programme started on this revolutionary design. Fords started off by building a further car with restyled bodywork which they intended to run as a Group 7 car in the Can-Am series. Tragedy disrupted this project – while testing the car at Riverside Raceway in August 1966 Ken Miles had a terrible high-speed crash which cost him his life. Despite the most thorough investigation, no satisfactory explanation was found – but it could have been a structural failure. By January 1967 Fords were again ready to test the latest version of the 'J'. This was now back in Group 6 Prototype trim and the tests carried out at Daytona Raceway proved two things. Firstly that in terms of both increased chassis rigidity and savings in weight the new car was a complete success, but that there were still aerodynamic problems to be solved.

By April and the Sebring 12-hours Fords considered the car raceworthy and it made its competition debut under the title Mk IV. The body had been completely restyled and the spare wheel was mounted vertically to the left of the gearbox and could be removed through a hatch in the tail. The supporting Mk IIs of the Ford team had also been modified. These were lighter than the 1966 cars and featured new fibreglass noses and tail sections, with re-positioned frontal air ducts. So-called 'turbine-styled' magnesium wheels of a new type were used, and these Mk II-Bs also had the spare wheel alongside the gearbox. On the Mk II-B this was removed through the rear of the tail. The improved Mk II did not appear until the Le Mans race.

Slough Support for the Ford Image

The reason why the latest Ford prototype was called the Mk IV was that the designation Mk III had been given to the latest development at Slough, where some big administrative changes had taken place. In late 1966 John Willment gave up entering his 'Race-proved by Willment' team of Ford-powered cars and with John Wyer formed a new Company known as JW Automotive Engineering Ltd. JW Automotive took over from Ford Advanced Vehicles their Slough works and responsibility for the manufacture of the road-going and Group 4 versions of the GT40. At the New York International Motor Show which opened on April 1st, 1967, there was announced the Mk III version of the GT40, redesigned to meet the new North American safety standards. Among the changes were a centrally mounted gear-lever, regulation height bumpers, increased luggage space and adjustable seats instead of the former adjustable pedals. Power output of the Ford 4·7-litre engine in normal production form was slightly reduced from 335 bhp at 6250 rpm to 306 bhp at 6000 rpm, but if the car was intended for competition use it could be supplied in a higher state of tune.

The production car represented only one side of the new concern's activities, for JW Automotive also built for the 1967 season a new prototype car sponsored by the Gulf Oil concern. This was basically a GT40, but incorporated a large number of minor chassis improvements which John Wyer had evolved, and had a new body style with reduced frontal area and distinguishable mainly by its different 'greenhouse' with sloping side-windows. At the Le Mans test weekend normal 4·7-litre engines were installed, but these were soon changed to units of just over 5 litres, and later in the season both cars had 5·7-litre engines developed by Holman and Moody. Wyer continued to use the ZF 5-speed gearbox as on the production cars. Very large disc brakes were fitted and the front ones had large flexible air hoses which led to aluminium 'muffs' over the braking surface. The cars were known as the 'Mirage' – one reason for the choice of the name was that it could be easily pronounced in any country – and were given a distinctive Gulf colour finish of pale blue with an orange stripe down the centre of the car. The team was then run on very much the same lines as had been the Essex Wire Corporation's team of GT40s in 1966, for John Wyer had been responsible for the preparation of these and they had the same team manager, David Yorke. Yorke is a particularly able and experienced man in this field with a vast amount of experience including responsibility for Tony Vandervell's Vanwall Grand Prix cars which won the Constructors' World Championship in 1958. Although the cars would never be fast enough to match the works Ferraris and Fords, they were clearly going to be a strong 'second-string' contender, but the change of name from Ford to Mirage was going to cause Dearborn a great deal of annoyance later in the season.

The Bearer of British Hopes

At Slough yet another project for prototype racing was under way, a project of Eric Broadley who had been the real father of the

Ford GT, in conjunction with John Surtees and Aston Martin Lagonda Ltd. Since his abrupt departure from the Ferrari team John Surtees has been driving for Honda. As the Japanese team engages only in Grand Prix racing, and as their headquarters in Europe are also at Slough, Surtees now has greater opportunities for co-operating in projects with Broadley and this arrangement works both ways, for the Honda which won the 1967 European Grand Prix had a chassis which was almost pure Lola in concept.

The Lola T70 which was entered in prototype events during 1967 was a direct development of the open Group 7 car which Broadley and Surtees had been racing since 1965. Powered by a mid-mounted Chevrolet engine, it had been one of the most successful cars of its type and had dominated, despite a strong challenge from Chaparral and McLaren, the 1966 Can-Am series. The chassis was a multi-tubular space frame structure with typical 'Grand Prix' wishbone suspension front and rear, and fitted with a Hewland 5-speed gearbox. The main chassis difference between the Group 7 car and the new prototype was that the new car had the now typical coupé bodywork, and apart from its dark green colour finish was difficult to distinguish at certain angles from the Ferrari P4.

The Aston Martin contribution to the project was the engine, which was a new 5064 cc (98 × 83 mm) V-8 design, a layout which Astons chose because of its advantages of good internal stressing and low weight. Even so, the new unit was not only massive-looking, but it weighed 525 lb, which was about the same as the 6-cylinder engine used in the production DB6 model. The engine had a light alloy cylinder block and twin overhead camshafts per bank of cylinders with four twin choke Weber carburettors in the vee of the engine and the exhaust manifolds outside the block. Dry sump lubrication was featured. By the Le Mans race Lucas fuel injection had been fitted to these cars.

From the moment it was exhibited at the racing car show in London in January 1967, doubts were expressed as to its potential. For Aston Martin's contribution to the project to be worthwhile, output would have to be 100 bhp per litre with complete reliability. But it seemed unlikely that much over 400 bhp was being pushed out by the unit and so it had little advantage over a well-developed American cast-iron V-8 production unit. Aston Martin's reputation as a builder of competition engines was not outstanding. The unit which had powered all their sports/racing models from the original

DB2 to the DBR1, the winner of the 1959 Sports Car World Championship, had been evolved from W. O. Bentley's original design for the Lagonda which had appeared in 1947. Throughout its career this engine had been inconsistent in performance – one example would be down on power and reliable, while another, to all intents and purposes identical, would give the intended power, but would be brittle and unreliable. The 4½-litre V-12 Lagonda which the team had raced during the 1954-55 seasons had never been right and Wyer had seemed unable to induce it to run on all 12 cylinders at once. When rumours spread that John Surtees had blown up two of the new V-8 engines in tests at Silverstone and would really have preferred to use Chevrolet engines at Le Mans, enthusiasts began to realise that the project was doomed to failure.

Daytona Continental

If Ferrari had learned one lesson from 1966, it was the foolishness of not entering at least one of the American events at the beginning of the season, thereby giving Ford a walkover. To remedy matters in 1967, extensive testing was carried out at Daytona before the race, and for the race itself Ferrari sent out two of the latest P4s driven by Mike Parkes and Lodovico Scarfiotti, and Lorenzo Bandini and Chris Amon. The talent of the young New Zealander had at last been properly recognised and his year with Ferrari was to give him plenty of work at the wheel of both Grand Prix cars and Prototypes. He is certainly among the best long-distance drivers, but later in the season he was to incur an admonishment from the Ferrari team manager for not flogging his Grand Prix cars hard enough, but driving them as though they had to last a race of prototype length. Backing up the works cars were the NART 'compromise' P3/4s shared by Pedro Rodriguez and Jean Guichet and Masten Gregory and Jo Schlesser, and an Ecurie Francorchamps car for Willy Mairesse and 'Beurlys'.

Fords were out in force with six cars, but, although these were not the latest models under development, they were newly-built Mk IIs with sundry detail modifications and the Shelby entries, especially, had an awful lot of handling problems to sort out in practice. The latest 2F Chaparral was driven by Phil Hill, but for the 1967 season he had a new co-driver, Mike Spence. Spence was a one-time Lotus works driver and for 1967 number two in the BRM team to Jackie

Stewart, and was another young driver of exceptional ability. Spence's ability has become rather under-rated, partly as a result of his stint in 1965 as the number two driver in the Lotus team to Jim Clark. The older 2D Chaparral was driven by the American pair Bob Johnson and Bruce Jennings, but both cars had the latest lightweight 7-litre aluminium engine. In practice, second fastest time was credited to this pair with the 2F, but in fact the time had been recorded by Jim Hall himself. Fastest of all was Dan Gurney with a Mk II Ford, whose time was an unofficial record-breaking 1 min 55·1 sec. Fastest of the Ferraris was Rodriguez with the NART car, who was third fastest of all, for the works cars were taking it easy, well aware from their earlier trials of the times they could achieve. No less than nine cars in practice beat the lap record set by Gurney in the 1966 race. Among other interesting entries were the GT40 entered by JW Automotive and driven by Jackie Ickx and Dick Thompson and the P2/3 Ferrari of David Piper which he shared with Dickie Attwood.

When the green flag dropped for the rolling start on the Saturday, straight into the lead went the 2F Chaparral with Phil Hill at the wheel. Lapping at over 112 mph, Hill gradually opened up a worthwhile gap between himself and the howling, pursuing pack of Fords and Ferraris. Soon the Fords began to have their troubles, Mario Andretti (co-driving with Richie Ginther) threw a tread on his Mk II and came in for all four wheels to be changed, a minor incident compared with the delay to the Mk II of Ronnie Bucknum (co-driving with Frank Gardner) who stopped with gearbox trouble. The mechanics changed the box, which took 28 minutes. At the end of the first hour the leading Chaparral had averaged 114·118 mph and the four untroubled Fords were ahead of all the Ferraris. The McLaren/Bianchi Ford ran into overheating problems during the second hour, caused by body parts that did not fit properly, and this plagued it for the rest of the race. The other Fords began to drop back and the Ferraris moved up. At the three hour mark Chaparral hopes were shattered when Phil Hill slid on some gravel and bounced off the retaining wall of the banking. Hill limped back to the pits, the rear suspension and chassis of the Chaparral damaged. A rear wishbone was changed, but the Chaparral retired after a couple of exploratory laps.

With the disappearance of the Chaparral, the Ferrari pit speeded up the cars and the works P4s went into the lead, while Ford after

Ford started to go into the pits with transmission trouble. The trouble was improperly machined gears and the remedy was to change the gearbox, but only a temporary remedy, as the new 'boxes had the same trouble. And gearbox trouble was not the only Ford worry, for the A. J. Foyt/Dan Gurney Ford had clutch and battery problems and the Donohue/Revson car had disappeared out on the track with shock-absorber failure. As the Fords came in and came out of their pit area chaos reigned, and in the words of one reporter, 'the tension was like the front line in Vietnam'. So many gearbox changes were made that the Ford pit counted nine and then lost track. The mechanics got in enough practice to reduce the time for a change down to 14 minutes, but then ran out of gearboxes. This made certain of the Ford defeat, unless all the Ferraris fell by the wayside and the two Fords, whose gearboxes had been replaced by the more reliable older type, survived.

At the half-way mark Bandini and Amon led Parkes and Scarfiotti. Third was the NART Ferrari of Rodriguez and Guichet. Despite this domination of the lead, Ferraris were not without their troubles. During the night hours the Piper privately-entered P2/3 fell back from sixth place with electrical problems and finally went out with noisy transmission indicative of imminent failure. Transmission failure also eliminated the Belgian Ferrari and the NART car of Schlesser and Gregory was pushed into the dead car park after water had started to run out of its exhausts. A tremendous dice for fourth place between the works 910 Porsche of Jo Siffert and Hans Herrmann and Charlie Kolb's privately-entered Dino was decided in favour of the Porsche when the Dino seized its engine on the banking. Another retirement was the Chaparral 2D which went out with transmission failure. By eight on the Sunday morning the Foyt/ Gurney Ford had staggered back to fourth spot, but it went out soon afterwards with a blown-up engine caused by oil starvation. During the last seven hours of the race no dramatic changes took place and the Ferraris were so securely esconced in the lead that they were able to reduce speed substantially and the race average dropped to 106·7 mph. Despite the need for frequent stops to take on water, the sole remaining Ford of McLaren and Bianchi was lapping fastest of all and rose to seventh place, which it retained to the finish. At 3 pm the Ferrari victory was settled by the chequered flag, a complete triumph that resulted from good organisation, a proper testing programme and a determination to make an impression on the

American racing scene, dominated by Ford for two seasons. Ford's trouncing, partly caused by a technical error, was partially compensated for by the JW Automotive GT40 taking sixth place and victory in its class, despite overheating and low oil pressure.

Sebring

Just under two months later the American teams reassembled in Florida for the Sebring 12-hours race. The Sebring course had been modified by rebuilding one of the most difficult corners into high-speed sweeps. Ferrari decided to give the race a miss and Ford turned up with only two cars, but one of these was the new Mk IV version driven by Bruce McLaren and Mario Andretti. The Chaparrals were as at Daytona. The rest of the field in this rather unexciting race was made up by the works Porsches, a pack of privately-entered Dinos and the works Alfa Romeo Tipo 33s, new 2-litre V-8 Prototypes making their race debut.

Fastest in practice was the new Mk IV Ford, with a time of 2 min 48 sec and the 2F Chaparral was only 2·6 seconds slower. This now had the wing fully adjustable, whereas it had been fixed at Daytona for straight-line running. Before the Sebring race, Spence had spent a test day at the circuit familiarising himself with use of the wing. When the race started the Chaparral was delayed with mechanical trouble and into the lead went the Alfa 33 of de Adamich. At the end of the first lap the Alfa still led, with the Dino owned and driven by Pedro Rodriguez close behind. Foyt (Mk II Ford) and McLaren (Mk IV) were next in line. McLaren did his second lap at 108·33 mph and a lap later was in the lead ahead of Foyt. An hour later the Fords still led, but soon they were in trouble of a minor nature, for the fuel pumps would not pick up the last ten gallons in the tanks. By quarter distance the Hall/Spence Chaparral had fought its way through the field to snatch a narrow lead from the Fords. Five laps later the Piper/Attwood P2/3 which had been in fourth place went out with a recurrence of its Daytona transmission trouble. All the privately-entered Dinos were in trouble of one sort or another and both the works Alfas had been eliminated by mechanical trouble after displaying tremendous speed. Mechanical trouble had also eliminated the 2D Chaparral, and despite its pace and the fact that it had set a new lap record of 111·03 mph (2 min 48·6 sec), the leading 2F was giving the pits a great deal of anxiety as it was smoking badly. The Chaparral fell back to second place behind the Mk IV Ford and shortly after dark was pushed away from the pits with gearbox failure caused by an oil leak.

The Fords thundered round, as unchallenged as had been the Ferraris at Daytona. Lying third was the flat-six Porsche 910 of Mitter and Patrick equally unchallenged in its class. Thirty minutes before the chequered flag the second-place Mk II of Foyt and Ruby rumbled into the pits with a very rough sounding engine. Up with the engine cover and a very quick diagnosis – a broken camshaft. The third-place Porsche began to close the gap, and when the flag fell it was not clear whether or not it had caught the stricken Ford. The timekeepers consulted with each other and decided that although the Porsche and the Ford had completed the same number of laps – 12 behind the winning Mk IV – the Ford was slightly ahead on the road. So Sebring was over with Fords' first victory of the season, a hollow win in the absence of Ferrari and a dull race after the retirement of the leading Chaparral.

The Monza 1000 *Kilometres Race*

Before the first prototype event of the European season Ferrari, Ford, Lola and Mirage all appeared at the Le Mans test week-end. On balance, the week-end provided little of interest. Ford, who had come with both Mk IIs and a Mk IV did not try very hard, as they were anxious to avoid a repetition of the previous year's disaster in which Walt Hansgen had lost his life. Nevertheless with speeds of around 204–206 mph they were faster down the Mulsanne Straight than the Ferraris, which were doing slightly under 200 mph. Fastest times of the week-end were by P4s driven by Bandini and Parkes at 3 min 25·5 sec (146·53 mph) and 3 min 27·6 sec. Surtees with the very pretty Lola-Aston Martin made third fastest time with 3 min 31·9. A rusty rear-engined Bizzarini turned up on a rusty lorry and despite its 5·3-litre Chevrolet engine was only two seconds faster than the works Mini-Marcos with a 1275S Cooper engine. One interesting car was the new Matra with a 4·7-litre Ford engine. This did 3 min 53·6 sec on the Saturday in the hands of Roby Weber, a talented but very excitable French driver. Later in the day Weber took out the Matra-BRM. The car snaked on the Mulsanne Straight, skidded and rolled and burst into flames. The driver died in the conflagration. What made it all the more tragic was that 27-year-old Weber was due to be married the following week.

The Monza race was contested by two works P4 Ferraris, the NART and Filipinetti P3/4s, the Mirages and a solitary 2F Chaparral. Although Chaparral had two cars entered at Le Mans, their policy was to enter one only (each car alternately) in the other prototype events. Right from the start the race developed into a furious fight between the two works Ferraris and the Chaparral, and Spence was driving superbly. He held second place behind Bandini's P4 until after the first hour's racing, when he stopped to investigate a peculiar vibration in the rear. It was found that a rear tyre was losing air, the wheel was changed, the car rejoined the race, but the vibration was still there. Back into the pits came the Chaparral, this time to stay there, for it was discovered that there was trouble with one of the drive-shafts.

The Bandini/Amon Ferrari was now way ahead of the rest of the field. The second works car came in with fuel pump trouble similar to that which had affected the Fords at Sebring. When Parkes rejoined the race, Pedro Rodriguez had closed up with his NART car. Parkes and Rodriguez fought it out side by side all round the circuit until lap 47, when Rodriguez tried to outbrake the works car as they went into the artificial chicane before the banking. The young Mexican misjudged the situation and clouted the barrier firmly, putting the NART car out of the race. The works Ferraris were now completely unchallenged and finished four laps ahead of the Porsche 910 of Rindt and Mitter. Fourth was the very battered Scuderia Filipinetti P3/4 which Vaccarella had clouted front and rear after missing a gearchange and spinning. The only Mirage to finish, driven by David Piper and Richard Thompson, was ninth after delays to cure a water leak and replace a broken damper. The other Slough car had retired with ignition trouble.

The Spa 1000 *Kilometres Race*

As the Spa race was held only a week after Monza it meant some very hurried preparation work. Ferrari entered only one works car, a P4 coupé identical to those he had run at Monza and driven by Mike Parkes and Scarfiotti; he was supported by the Équipe Nationale Belge car of Mairesse and 'Beurlys' and the Maranello Concessionaires entry for Attwood and Lucien Bianchi. The solitary

Chaparral was again driven by Hill and Spence; the two Mirages were entered, that of the young Belgian driver Jackie Ickx and Alan Rees having a brand new 5·7-litre Holman and Moody engine. Of particular interest were two brand new Lola T70 Mk III coupés, exactly as entered by the works at Le Mans, except they were powered by Chevrolet V-8 engines. One of these, however, was crashed in practice by Mike de Udy and did not start.

When the race started at 1 pm on the Monday the circuit had already been completely soaked by heavy rain that showed no signs of abating. Hall instructed his Chaparral drivers to take it easy and not to use the wing, which had not yet been tested in wet conditions. While Ickx and Mairesse, taking full advantage of their knowledge of the circuit, went into the lead, the Maranello car stalled on the grid and joined the race three minutes in arrears. Piper crashed the Mirage with the 4·7 litre engine, but team-mate Ickx continued to dominate the race. The Chaparral was eliminated by transmission trouble, but not before Spence had had the chance, in slightly improved conditions, to use the wing. With the wing in the fixed position, the Chaparral suffered a severe drag which reduced speed by 12 to 15 mph, but using the wing properly Spence set the fastest lap of the race. The works Ferrari was well down the field after delays to sort out a top gear that would not engage properly, and Mairesse pranged the second-place Ferrari.

While Ickx, with Dick Thompson as co-driver after the elimination of the other Mirage, had a clear lap's lead with the race three-quarters run, a battle for second place raged between Siffert's Porsche, Attwood's Ferrari, which had made up enough ground to be in the hunt, Parkes with the works Ferrari and the Lola with Paul Hawkins at the wheel. The eventual finishing order was:

1st J. Ickx/R. Thompson (Mirage)
2nd J. Siffert/H. Herrmann (Porsche 910)
3rd R. Attwood/L. Bianchi (Ferrari P3/4)
4th P. Hawkins/J. Epstein (Lola)
5th M. Parkes/L. Scarfiotti (Ferrari P4)
6th P. Sutcliffe/B. Redman (Ford GT40)

Although the Ferrari team returned to Maranello thoroughly beaten, they had been beaten, not by a better car, but by their own mechanical failings and the superior knowledge of a difficult, soaking wet course by a local driver. Once again Ferrari had paid the price for entering only one car in an important race. Unfortunately for Ford, because of the change of name and mechanical modifications of the Mirage, the FIA would not allow the win to count as part of Ford's Championship points.

The Targa Florio

It was an even sadder Ferrari team that went to Sicily for the Targa Florio held on May 14th. The previous week-end Lorenzo Bandini had crashed his V-12 Ferrari in the Monaco Grand Prix. Trapped beneath his blazing car, which was not fitted with a roll-over bar, and with rescue work hampered by the refusal of the organisers to stop the race, he had suffered severe burns from which he died shortly afterwards in hospital. Not the most placid of the leading Grand Prix drivers, Bandini took his racing and his patriotism a bit too seriously for many tastes. He drove with tremendous enthusiasm and force and possessed a greater appreciation for the mechanics of his car than many drivers. He was probably the last of the long line of temperamental, highly talented Italian drivers and his loss to Ferrari was immeasurable.

Only one works P4 for Vaccarella and Scarfiotti was entered in the Targa Florio, together with an 18-valve Dino for Günther Klass and Casoni. The Scuderia Filipinetti also entered their P3/4 for Müller and Guichet. Chaparral had entered one car for fun, knowing that they had little chance of victory, anxious not to prang the car with Le Mans so close and competing because they felt that their European season would not be complete without the Targa Florio. One of the highlights of the trip were the antics of the Sicilian crowd when Hill sat in the stationary Chaparral and operated the wing. At first the crowd fled, but curiosity overcame them and they returned to stand and stare, not really sure whether the wing had moved or not and fearful lest it should move again. For, familiar though they were with the sight of a Ferrari or a Porsche, the Chaparral was something beyond their comprehension. Strong contenders for victory came from Porsche with three of the 910s with space-frame chassis, 2·2-litre 8-cylinder engines and Bosch fuel injection, and three similar cars with 6-cylinder fuel-injection engines. Alfa Romeo had entered three of the Tipo 33s but they were having trouble with the front suspension collapsing.

Fastest in practice and favourite with the locals was Nino

Vaccarella, but he did an unexpected silly on the first lap of the hot and dusty race and wrecked the P4 against a stone wall. The Filipinetti Ferrari went out with transmission failure. The Chaparral punctured a rear tyre, and as the spare wheel would fit the front only, Hap Sharp was forced to retire. The works Dino was pranged against a bridge and the leading Alfa 33 in the 2-litre class, driven by de Adamich and Rolland, did as expected and broke its front suspension – as a safety precaution a wire-cage device had been attached to the Alfas to prevent the hub leaving the car altogether when the suspension broke! Despite several of their cars crashing, works Porsches occupied the first three places, led home by the 2·2-litre car of Paul Hawkins and Stommelen. Fourth home was the privately-entered Dino of Venturi who had as a co-driver the young Englishman, Jonathan Williams. Williams was officially a Ferrari works team driver, but Enzo very rarely gave him a drive. The Porsche victory was their fourth in seven years.

The Nürburgring 1000 Kilometres Race

Ford had not competed in a European race during the 1967 season, conserving all their efforts for Le Mans, and it could be argued with justification that they cannot claim to have dominated prototype racing until they have won the Targa Florio and the Nürburgring race, for these are equally testing, albeit in different ways. Equally busy with his preparations for Le Mans, Ferrari sent no P4s to the Nürburgring, but only a token entry consisting of a Dino with a 2·4-litre V-6 engine which was basically what he had been using in Grand Prix racing eight years previously. This was driven by Scarfiotti and Klass and Scuderia Filipinetti borrowed a works 18-valve Dino. Neither started, as the 2·4-litre broke its engine and the other Dino caught fire and was burnt out. Another casualty in practice was the Mirage of Dick Thompson, which had a new 5-litre Ford engine developed by the Gurney-Weslake 'Eagle' organisation. This was badly crashed, but the driver was not hurt.

This left the remaining Mirage of Ickx and Attwood, the Chaparral of Spence and Hill and the Lola-Aston Martin, making its race debut, to battle with a total of six works Porsches, and most people favoured the Porsches. Spence, with the Chaparral, was fastest in practice with a time of 8 min 31·9 sec over a circuit which had been modified since the 1966 race. This modification took the form of an

S-bend, adding 25 metres to the length of the circuit, and was done to slow the cars off before they breasted the *Tiergarten* hump. At the other end of the scale of the 69 starters was a Honda S800 coupé exactly four minutes slower than the Chaparral, and this gives a fair idea of the dangerous speed differentials on this circuit.

At the Le Mans-type start, both Lola and Chaparral got left behind. Surtees had difficulty in getting the engine to start and Hill was caught up in the Chaparral's safety harness. Once he finally sorted himself out Hill tore through the field passing cars on the left and right and diving between pairs of them. By lap 9 he was in the lead but at the end of that lap went into the pits complaining about a rumble in the transmission. Spence took over after the car had been refuelled, and after the engine had stalled twice, moved away, but came to rest at the first corner after the pits, with the transmission making a tearing and grinding noise. Surtees had already disappeared from the circuit in a dramatic and frightening manner. When in eighth place on lap 8, he was plunging down that part of the circuit known as the *Fuchsröhe*, flat out in top gear, a rear wishbone broke and the car slid violently from one side of the track to the other as Surtees fought for control. At the bottom of the hill he brought the car to rest, having only just missed an abandoned Porsche by the roadside. The Mirage never rose above fifth place and eventually retired out on the circuit with both offside tyres punctured. As was not unexpected Porsche dominated the race, taking the first four and sixth places and split by the sole surviving member of the Alfa Romeo Tipo 33 team.

Le Mans

With a renewal of the battle between the two main contenders and strong outsiders in the shape of the Chaparral, Mirage and Lola, there was every prospect of the 1967 Le Mans race being one of the best in the series, and every possibility of one of the outsiders scoring an unexpected win.

Having led at Daytona, set fastest lap at Spa and led at the Nurburgring, the Chaparral was the fastest of the 'big bangers', but it was constantly having trouble with its automatic transmission. If Hall and Sharp had cured this trouble, it could well win, for in all other respects it was completely reliable. At Le Mans the cars were driven by Hill and Spence, who had a new, lighter and more powerful alloy engine, and Johnson and Jennings. Both Chaparrals had twin choke carburettors which were an exact copy of those made by Weber. Hall's tactics were that Hill and Spence would 'tiger' with the Fords and Ferraris and if the opposition were broken, the second car could then move up.

Completely untested in open racing was the Lola, for at the Nurbürgring Surtees had not lasted long enough to display its capabilities. Both cars at Le Mans had Lucas fuel injection and Surtees' co-driver was David Hobbs. Surtees' car was a brand new one with an adjustable spoiler across the tail. The older car was driven by Chris Irwin and South African driver Peter de Klerk.

Both Mirages had 5·7-litre Holman and Moody engines and were driven by David Piper and Dick Thompson and Jackie Ickx and Brian Muir. Their victory at Spa had been exceptional and was a result mainly of Ickx's intimate knowledge of the circuit. They were unlikely to do well unless all the faster cars broke.

From Ford came a total of seven superbly prepared 7-litre cars made up as follows:

Entered by Shelby American Inc.:
Dan Gurney/A. J. Foyt (red Mk IV)
Bruce McLaren/Mark Donohue (yellow Mk IV)
Paul Hawkins/Ronnie Bucknum (light blue Mk II)
Entered by Holman and Moody Inc.:
Lucien Bianchi/Mario Andretti (bronze Mk IV)
Dennis Hulme/Lloyd Ruby (dark blue Mk IV)
Frank Gardner/Roger McClusky (gold Mk II)
Prepared by Holman and Moody and entered by Ford-France:
Jo Schlesser/Guy Ligier (white Mk II)

Anthony Joseph Foyt, Junior, of Houston, Texas, but preferring to be known simply as A. J. Foyt, was the most remarkable driver in the Ford team, for he has had outstanding success both at Indianapolis and in European-type events. At the age of 32, he had just won the 1967 '500' race, his third victory in the event which he had also won in 1961 and 1964. He is the epitome of the American professional driver and regards his racing as an immensely complex job which he does to the best of his professional ability. Thirty-year-old Mark Donohue is an engineer by profession and has raced a wide range of cars from the Elva with which he won his first SCCA Championship in 1961, to midget racing cars and Cobras. Another very fast member of the Ford team was the light-hearted 29-year-old Australian Paul Hawkins, one of the most conscientious drivers, who concealed his seriousness of purpose beneath a facade of flippancy and humour. He had driven for John Willment from 1963 to 1965 and during 1967 scored a large number of successes with his own GT40. Frank Gardner was another Australian, aged 34, and a very skilled mechanic as well as driver. He too had raced cars for John Willment and was a steady and experienced team-member who could be relied upon to keep his head in any circumstances.

In all their previous clashes, Ferrari had been outweighed in numbers by the Ford team, but he came to Le Mans in 1967 with a total of seven cars, three in the name of the works and four entered by his supporting teams. This is how the Ferrari entries looked:

Entered by SEFAC. Ferrari (the initials stand for 'Societa per Azioni Esercizio Fabbriche Automobile e Corse):
P4s for Mike Parkes and Lodovico Scarfiotti, Günther Klass and Peter Sutcliffe (Sutcliffe was a very experienced driver who raced his own GT40), Chris Amon and Nino Vaccarella.
Entered by Équipe Nationale Belge:
P4 loaned by the works and driven by Willy Mairesse and 'Beurlys'.
Entered by Maranello Concessionaires Ltd:
P3/4 for Dick Attwood and Piers Courage.
Entered by Scuderia Filipinetti:
P3/4 for Hans Müller and Jean Guichet.
Entered by the North American Racing Team:
P3/4 for Pedro Rodriguez and Giancarlo Baghetti.

All the Dinos and the Tipo 33 Alfas were scratched before the race, so the 2-litre class was a Porsche benefit unless the Matras could intervene. Dominating the Wednesday and Thursday practice sessions was Phil Hill with the Chaparral, who got down to 3 min 24·7 sec on the second night. By a supreme all-stops-out effort on the Thursday after darkness had fallen McLaren managed to beat the Chaparral with a frighteningly fast lap of 3 min 24·4 sec (147 mph). All the other Fords and all the Ferraris were decidedly slower, the best Ferrari time being seventh fastest by Parkes with 3 min 28·9 sec. Practice was not without troubles for both teams, as Fords were having windscreens blow out and this meant ferrying new assemblies from the States and Ferrari had to repair the P4 which Klass crashed when a slower car crossed his line through a corner.

A worthwhile safety introduction for this race was the use of coloured discs on the side of the body to identify the material used, i.e. yellow for aluminium, red for fibreglass, blue for steel and green for magnesium. When coping with an accident, marshals could easily identify from these 3 in. wide luminous discs the material they had to deal with. The Fords, Ferraris and Porsches were fitted with numbered discs coated with phosphorous and incorporating an electrical circuit coupled to the alternator. In the dark, the disc glowed green, with the black number standing out against it. When the current was switched off in daylight the disc was white.

The Saturday was dull and overcast, and when the starting signal was given to the 54 starters, the Mk II of Bucknum went into a lead, which it held for over an hour. As was almost inevitable the Chaparrals were left on the starting line, and had to try and make up lost time as best they could. Surtees retired his Lola after three laps with piston failure and the second car followed soon afterwards with a broken camshaft. So much for the Aston Martin engine!

Both Mirages were soon in the pits with engine trouble and neither lasted long. During the second hour Bucknum's Ford split a water joint. After a pit stop for repairs, it was forced to crawl round until it had covered the necessary laps before water could be taken on. By 6 pm the order was Ford (Gurney/Foyt) – Chaparral (Hill/Spence) – Ford (Bianchi/Andretti) – Ford (McLaren/Donohue) – Ferrari (Parkes/Scarfiotti) – Ferrari (Mairesse/'Beurlys') – Ferrari (Amon/Vaccarella). Already the Italian cars were being outpaced and Denis Hulme, anxious to make up time for an excursion into a sand bank, set up a searing new lap record of 3 min 23·6 sec (148·7 mph). Two hours later at 8 pm the leading Chaparral had dropped a place and then was forced to make a pit stop lasting nine minutes for work on the automatic transmission – once again the Achilles heel of the Chaparral was bringing about its downfall. Amon's Ferrari burst a tyre and as he limped back to the pits the car suddenly caught fire and was completely burnt out. Just before 11 pm Lloyd Ruby stuffed the lap-record-breaking Ford into a sandbank and was forced to abandon it. The slower of the Chaparrals was eliminated by electrical trouble and the Hill/Spence car had lost control of its wing, which reduced its top speed. By midnight Gurney/Foyt and McLaren/Donohue led the Ferrari of Parkes and Scarfiotti. The Ford of Bianchi and Andretti was fourth, but overtook the Ferrari during the next hour. The Fords were clearly running to a carefully timed pattern and although anything could – and did – go wrong, at this stage in the race they could not be better placed.

During the early hours of the Sunday morning both sides took a sickening blow. The Ferraris of Scuderia Filipinetti and NART retired with engine failure, the first with no oil and the second with oil in all the wrong places. Shortly afterwards the yellow danger light went out and the Ford pit started wondering where all their cars had disappeared to. Jo Schlesser of the Ford-France car which had been sixth behind the Chaparral came in with the story that there had been Fords all over the road, and he had had to hit the bank to miss them. Bit by bit the facts emerged. Andretti had a brake lock as he went into the Esses and smashed into the bank. McClusky tried to avoid him and hit the other bank. Schlesser came on to the scene, managed to avoid both cars, but hit the bank himself. As McLaren was forced to make a pit stop for attention to the clutch, the whole face of the race had changed. Ford held a tenuous lead with the Gurney/Foyt car, the Parkes/Scarfiotti Ferrari was second and the Chaparral third.

As dawn broke at 4 am only 37 cars were left running and many more were to retire. The Maranello Concessionaires P3 expired with piston ring failure. The Chaparral came into the pits with oil running out of the automatic transmission through a broken seal. Hall and the mechanics started to replace the seal, reckoning it would be a two hour job. It took nearly three hours, the car rejoined the race in 17th position and retired an hour afterwards with the transmission broken. Although at 6 am the leading Ford had a six-lap lead, the Ferraris in second, third and fourth places were all healthy, still had an excellent chance and were being driven flat out in an attempt to catch the leader. Four hours later there had been no change in the leading positions, but McLaren came into the pits with the engine cover missing. Immediately he was sent out to look for it, eventually found it and came back to the pits where the tail of the car was patched up with leather belts and masking tape. Shortly afterwards the Klass/Sutcliffe car retired with a sheared injection pump drive and the Hawkins/Bucknum Ford broke its engine.

So the race drew to a close with the two red Ferraris howling round in vain pursuit of the leading Ford and praying that something on the Ford would break. For the whole 24 hours this race was run flat out with none of the usual easing off as it drew to a close. Nothing broke on the Ford and Foyt and Gurney came home the winners, having smashed the race average. They had covered 3250 miles, and their average speed of 132·49 mph was over 6 mph better than the speed in 1966.

1967

RESULTS

1st A. J. Foyt/D. Gurney (Ford Mk IV) – 132·49 mph
2nd M. Parkes/L. Scarfiotti (Ferrari P4)
3rd W. Mairesse/'Beurlys' (Ferrari P4)
4th B. McLaren/M. Donohue (Ford Mk IV)
5th J. Siffert/H. Herrmann (Porsche 907)
6th R. Stommelen/J. Neerpasch (Porsche 910)
7th V. Elford/B. Pon (Porsche 906)
8th G. Koch/C. Poirot (Porsche 906)
9th H. Grandsire/J. Rosinsky (Alpine-Renault)
10th A. de Cortanze/A. Le Guellec (Alpine-Renault)
11th G. Steinemann/D. Spoerry (Ferrari 275GTB)
12th R. de Lageneste/J. Cheinisse (Alpine-Renault)
13th J. Vinatier/M. Bianchi (Alpine-Renault)
14th R. Buchet/H. Linge (Porsche 911S)
15th C. Baker/A. Hedges (Austin-Healey Sprite)
16th M. Martin/J. Mesange (Abarth OT1300)

The Siffert/Herrmann Porsche won the Index of Performance
Fastest lap was by Denis Hulme and Mario Andretti
in 3 min 23·6 sec (147·9 mph)

Ford had gained a well-deserved victory through careful preparation and the resultant reliability, through a sound choice of drivers, through their speed and through their numbers. The Ferrari team were delighted with their second and third places. They had hoped, but never expected to win. The P4s, as practice had clearly revealed, were just not fast enough, although they were much more reliable than the 1966 cars. Another consolation for Ferrari was that the 275GTB entered by the Scuderia Filipinetti had won the production Grand Touring category (Group 3 cars, more than 500 produced). Chaparral still had to sort out their transmission problems if they hoped to be successful. Lola had to scrap the Aston Martin engine if *they* hoped to succeed.

Later in the European Season

To round off the European season there were still to be held three International races for Prototypes. The first of these was the Rheims 12-hours race held in July and this saw a resurgence of Lola efforts. A total of four cars were entered including a works entry from Lola Racing. All had Chevrolet engines of various capacities, including the works car which was the newer of the two that had run at Le Mans. Facing these was a Mk II Ford entry from Ford-France and this in fact was the car which Paul Hawkins and Ronnie Bucknum had driven at Le Mans, but since then it had been flown to the States for a major overhaul and flown back again. All the Lolas retired and the Ford-France car won easily, seven laps ahead of David Piper's P2/3 Ferrari which he shared with Jo Siffert. Twelve minutes before the end of the race the Ferrari had thrown a connecting rod leaving an eight inch wide hole in the crankcase. Siffert had clanked his way back to the pits and after a cursory examination limped round for a final lap and across the finishing line when the flag fell.

Held at Brands Hatch at the end of July, the BOAC '500' was Britain's best motor race for many years, but even so was but a pale shadow of the sort of race held on the Continent. For Brands Hatch is a tiddling little circuit compared with Le Mans, Rheims or the Nurbürgring and with totally inadequate pits. Nevertheless its narrowness and twists and turns made it an exciting race for the drivers of the bigger cars who found themselves with power to spare and the problem of lapping slower cars much more frequently than on the longer Continental circuits. Chaparral had sent one car back to the States in preparation for the Can-Am series, but the other was present as usual with Spence and Phil Hill at the wheel. A rare sight in Britain were the works Prototype Ferraris of which three were fielded for Paul Hawkins and Jonathan Williams, Scarfiotti and Sutcliffe, and Jackie Stewart and Chris Amon. Stewart was driving a Ferrari for the first time and he enjoyed every moment of it. A sad loss to the Ferrari team and one of several which they had suffered during the 1967 season was the disablement of Parkes. He had been badly injured in a crash at the Belgian Grand Prix the week after Le Mans. Facing the Chaparral and Ferraris were a strong team of Porsches, a solitary Mirage and three Lola-Chevrolets.

Fastest in practice was the Chaparral with a time of 1 min 37·4 sec and the Lola Racing entry of Surtees/Hobbs and Sid Taylor's Lola driven by Dennis Hulme and Jack Brabham were next fastest. With 36 starters the course seemed crowded with cars and there were many minor shunts and one or two of the slower cars were pushed off the course as the faster boys elbowed their way into the corners. At the end of the first hour the Chaparral led from two P4s and at the finish five hours later still led with the Stewart/Amon Ferrari in second place and on the same lap. The average speed of the winning car was 93·08 mph. This success was a joy and inspiration to all concerned with the Chaparral, for they had the fastest car and they had been so close to victory all season, yet, because of mechanical unreliability, it had eluded them. Until this race one point had separated Ferrari and Porsche in the Prototype Championship and Maranello's placing in this race was sufficient to clinch it in their favour.

In the final non-Championship event of the season, the Paris 1000 kms race at Montlhéry on October 15th, victory went to the Mirage of Jackie Ickx and Paul Hawkins. The Équipe Nationale Belge Ferrari P3/4 of Mairesse and 'Beurlys' was second. A Porsche was third and the Ford-France Mk II 7-litre took fourth place.

So came the end of another tumultuous season of prototype racing, a season that would not be repeated. Shortly after the Le Mans race Fords had announced that they would not be competing in Europe in 1968. Whatever may be felt about the ethics of Ford domination of racing at such colossal expense, it must be conceded that their duel with Ferrari gave Prototype racing an impact and interest that would never otherwise have been attained.

Postscript

The day after the 1967 Le Mans race the Commission Sportive of the Federation Internationale de l'Automobile, a body formed of the men supposedly representing the motor sporting interests of their countries, voted that in 1968 Group 6 prototype cars would be limited to 3 litres and Group 4 cars to 5 litres. This decision was made without any of the representatives, who included Dean Delamont, Competitions Secretary of the Royal Automobile Club, consulting any of the interested race organisers or constructors. No satisfactory explanation of why he voted for the 3-litre limit has been made by Delamont and he has endeavoured to placate, without success, the motor sporting world with the excuse that the item appeared on the agenda at the last moment and with insufficient time for consultations.

The decision has been universally condemned by organisers and constructors including Porsche who have a vested interest in small capacity cars. It has meant the probable shelving of prototype projects by Aston Martin and Jaguar who are both believed to be working on competition cars with a capacity of approximately 5 litres. Chaparral have announced that the decision will render it impossible for them to compete in Europe in 1968.

What caused the item to appear on the agenda? The Automobile Club de l'Ouest, organisers of the Le Mans race, were well aware that the French Alpine concern, with financial backing from Renault, were building a prototype of 3 litres capacity and nothing would delight the French more than to see one of their own cars win on the Sarthe circuit. Furthermore it is probable that the French Club were already aware of Fords' decision, made public only after the CSI had met, not to compete in European racing in 1968. In this way they were able to sponsor their own projects without offending Ford or Ferrari, for Enzo would have no difficulty in building a 3-litre prototype, possibly based on the existing Dino.

The AC de l'Ouest had very close association with the Automobile Club de France, the French equivalent of the Royal Automobile Club. As the headquarters of the FIA are in Paris, it was natural that members of the ACF should hold important posts with the FIA and that there should be close ties between the two organisations. When the Le Mans Club, through this chain of relationships was able to impose their desire for a 3-litre Prototype limit on the motor sporting world, another French organisation became very angry. This was the Federation Francaise Sport Automobile (FFSA), a new club formed by competitors, organisers and constructors; they were tired of the antiquated thinking of the ACF whose attitudes appear to differ little from those they held at the turn of the Century. Already the FFSA had obtained a Government permission to deal with certain aspects of the sport, such as issuing licenses and race permits, but after the 3-litre limit was announced, they obtained Government support for their claim that they should represent French motor sporting interests at the FIA instead of the Automobile Club de France. Already in 1967 this application has been rejected by the FIA. The natural reaction of the FIA was to refuse to recognise the new body and for a while it looked as though this would affect the International standing of French motor sporting events. Happily the FIA have now relented and have agreed to recognise the FFSA as the French representative body. Although this appears to be nothing more than an internal wrangle, it will have the effect of preventing any undesirable changes, or changes at too short notice, in International racing that might have emanated from France.

Although there will no longer be a tumultuous clash in Prototype racing to match that of the Ford Versus Ferrari battle, the racing will continue to be exciting and inspiring. Although Ford participation will be restricted to the private teams Group 4 GT40s and Ferrari's new team manager Franco Gozzi has announced that the Maranello team will be building no new Group 4 or 6 cars for 1968, there will be clashes between the very fast and reliable Porsches (now in full 3-litre form), the French Matras and Alpines, and the Mirages. Mirage, like several other constructors, will be using the new 3-litre V-12 BRM engine and there will be the new Healey SR with a V-8 2-litre Coventry-Climax engine. Racing may have its ups and downs, but new constructors come to replace the old and for the enthusiast there is always plenty of excitement.

Appendix 1

The Performances of Works Ferraris in Sports Car Racing, 1964–67

Event	Results	
1964		
Sebring 12 hours, 22nd March	1st 2nd 3rd	M. Parkes/U. Maglioli (275/P), 93.36 mph L. Scarfiotti/N. Vaccarella (275/P) J. Surtees/L. Bandini (330/P)
Nurbürgring 1000 km, 31st May	1st Ret.	L. Scarfiotti/N. Vaccarella (275/P), 87·30 mph J. Surtees/L. Bandini (275/P) – rear axle-shaft failure
Le Mans 24 hours, 20th–21st June	1st 3rd Ret. Ret.	J. Guichet/N. Vaccarella (275/P), 121·55 mph J. Surtees/L. Bandini (330/P) M. Parkes/L. Scarfiotti (275/P) – suspected broken piston G. Baghetti/U. Maglioli (275/P) – crash
1965 Monza 1000 km, 25th April	1st 2nd Ret.	M. Parkes/J. Guichet (275/P2), 125·90 mph J. Surtees/L. Scarfiotti (330/P2) L. Bandini/N. Vaccarella (330/P2) – rear suspension failure
Targa Florio 9th May	1st Ret. Ret.	N. Vaccarella/L. Bandini (275/P2), 63·73 mph L. Scarfiotti/M. Parkes (275/P2) – crash J. Guichet/G. Baghetti (275/P2) – battery
Nurbürgring 1000 km, 23rd May	1st 2nd	J. Surtees/L. Scarfiotti (330/P2), 90·66 mph M. Parkes/J. Guichet (275/P2)

APPENDIX 1 157

Le Mans 24 hours, 19th–20th June	Ret. Ret. Ret.	J. Surtees/L. Scarfiotti (330/P2) – gearbox failure L. Bandini/G. Biscaldi (275/P2) – engine trouble M. Parkes/J. Guichet (330/P2) – engine trouble	
1966 Sebring 12 hours, 26th March	Ret.	M. Parkes/R. Bondurant (P3) – gearbox failure	
Monza 1000 km, 25th April	1st	J. Surtees/M. Parkes (P3), 110·45 mph	
Targa Florio, 8th May	Ret.	N. Vaccarella/L. Bandini (P3) – crash	
Spa 1000 km, 22nd May	1st	M. Parkes/L. Scarfiotti (P3), 126·43 mph	
Nürburgring 1,000 km, 5th June	Ret.	J. Surtees/M. Parkes (P3)	
Le Mans 24 hours, 18th–19th June	Ret. Ret.	M. Parkes/L. Scarfiotti (P3) – crash L. Bandini/J. Guichet (P3) – overheating	
1967 Daytona Continental 24 hours, 5th February	1st 2nd	L. Bandini/C. Amon (P4), 105·70 mph M. Parkes/L. Scarfiotti (P4)	
Monza 1000 km, 25th April	1st 2nd	L. Bandini/C. Amon (P4), 126·10 mph M. Parkes/L. Scarfiotti (P4)	

Event	Results	
Spa 1000 km, 1st May	5th	M. Parkes/L. Scarfiotti (P4)
Targa Florio, 14th May	Ret.	N. Vaccarella/L. Scarfiotti (P4) – crash
Le Mans, 10th–11th June	2nd	M. Parkes/L. Scarfiotti (P4)
	Ret.	G. Klass/P. Sutcliffe (P4) – sheared injector pump
	Ret.	C. Amon/N. Vaccarella (P4) – engine failure
BOAC 500, Brands Hatch, 30th July	2nd	J. Stewart/C. Amon (P4)
	5th	L. Scarfiotti/P. Sutcliffe (P4)
	6th	P. Hawkins/J. Williams (P4)

Appendix 2

The Performances of Works Fords in Sports Car Racing, 1964–67

Event	Results	
1964		
Nurbürgring 1000 km, 31st May	Ret.	P. Hill/B. McLaren (FAV) – rear suspension failure
Le Mans 24 hours, 20th–21st June	Ret.	R. Attwood/J. Schlesser (FAV) – fire caused by broken fuel line
	Ret.	R. Ginther/M. Gregory (FAV) – gearbox trouble
	Ret.	P. Hill/B. McLaren (FAV) – gearbox trouble

APPENDIX 2

Rheims 12 hours, 5th July	Ret. Ret. Ret.	R. Ginther/M. Gregory (FAV) – crown wheel and pinion failure R. Attwood/J. Schlesser (FAV) – gearbox trouble P. Hill/B. McLaren (FAV) – engine failure
1965 Daytona Continental 2000 km, 28th February	1st 3rd	K. Miles/L. Ruby (SA), 99·9 mph R. Ginther/R. Bondurant (SA)
Sebring 12 hours, 27th March	2nd Ret.	B. McLaren/K. Miles (SA) P. Hill/R. Ginther (SA) – fractured spring mounting
Monza 1000 km, 25th April	3rd Ret.	B. McLaren/K. Miles (SA) C. Amon/U. Maglioli (SA) – collapsed front suspension
Targa Florio, 9th May	Ret.	J. Whitmore/R. Bondurant (FAV) – crash
Nurbürgring 1000 km, 23rd May	8th Ret. Ret. Ret.	C. Amon/B. McLaren/P. Hill (SA) P. Hill/B. McLaren (SA) – broken drive-shaft R. Attwood/J. Whitmore (FAV) – broken engine bearers M. Trintignant/G. Ligier (FF) – broken engine bearers
Le Mans 24 hours, 19th–20th June	Ret. Ret. Ret. Ret.	K. Miles/B. McLaren (7-litre) (SA) – gearbox failure P. Hill/C. Amon (7-litre) (SA) – gearbox failure J. Whitmore/I. Ireland (FAV) – overheating M. Trintignant/G. Ligier (FF) – engine trouble

Event	Results	
1966 (All cars raced were the 7-litre Mk II model except where indicated)		
Daytona Continental 24 hours, 6th February	1st 2nd 3rd 5th	K. Miles/L. Ruby (SA), 109 mph D. Gurney/J. Grant (SA) W. Hansgen/M. Donohue (H & M) B. McLaren/C. Amon (SA)
Sebring 12 hours, 26th March	1st 2nd 12th Ret. Ret. Ret.	K. Miles/L. Ruby (SA), 98·07 mph W. Hansgen/M. Donohue (H & M) A. J. Foyt/R. Bucknum (H & M) D. Gurney/J. Grant (SA) – disqualified J. Whitmore/F. Gardner (4·7-litre) (AM) – clutch failure G. Hill/J. Stewart (4·7-litre) (AM) – engine trouble
Spa 1000 km, 22nd May	2nd	J. Whitmore/F. Gardner (AM)
Le Mans 24 hours, 18th–19th June	1st 2nd 3rd Ret. Ret. Ret. Ret. Ret.	B. McLaren/C. Amon (SA), 126·01 mph K. Miles/D. Hulme (SA) R. Bucknum/R. Hutcherson (H & M) P. Hawkins/M. Donohue (H & M) – differential failure J. Whitmore/F. Gardner (AM) – clutch failure L. Bianchi/M. Andretti (H & M) – engine failure G. Hill/B. Muir (AM) – suspension failure D. Gurney/J. Grant (SA) – overheating
1967 Daytona Continental	7th	B. McLaren/L. Bianchi (SA, Mk II)

APPENDIX 2

24 hours, 5th February	Ret.	M. Andretti/R. Ginther (H & M, Mk II) – gearbox failure
	Ret.	R. Bucknum/F. Gardner (H & M, Mk II) – gearbox failure
	Ret.	M. Donohue/P. Revson (H & M, Mk II) – gearbox failure
	Ret.	L. Ruby/D. Hulme (SA, Mk II) – gearbox failure
	Ret.	A. J. Foyt/D. Gurney (SA, Mk II) – engine failure
Sebring 12 hours, 1st April	1st	B. McLaren/M. Andretti (SA, Mk IV), 103·13 mph
	2nd	A. J. Foyt/L. Ruby (SA, Mk II)
Le Mans 24 hours, 10th–11th June	1st	A. J. Foyt/D. Gurney (SA, Mk IV), 132·49 mph
	4th	B. McLaren/M. Donohue (SA, Mk II)
	Ret.	P. Hawkins/R. Bucknum (SA, Mk II) – engine trouble
	Ret.	L. Bianchi/M. Andretti (H & M, Mk IV) – crash
	Ret.	D. Hulme/L. Ruby (H & M, Mk IV) – crash
	Ret.	F. Gardner/R. McClusky (H & M, Mk II) – crash
	Ret.	J. Schlesser/G. Ligier (FF, Mk II) – crash
Rheims 12 hours,	1st	J. Schlesser/G. Ligier (FF, Mk II), 127·54 mph

Note in the above:
SA = entered by Shelby American Inc.
FAV = entered by Ford Advanced Vehicles Ltd.
H & M = entered by Holman & Moody Inc.
AM = entered by Alan Mann Racing Ltd.
FF = entered by Ford-France.

Appendix 3

Specification of the Ferrari 275LM and P4

	275LM	P4
Engine		
Capacity:	3286 cc	3968 cc
Bore:	77 mm	77 mm
Stroke:	58.8 mm	71 mm
No. of cylinders:	12 in 60-degree vee formation	12 in 60-degree vee formation
Carburation:	Six twin-choke Weber	Lucas fuel injection
Valve operation:	Single overhead camshaft per bank of cylinders	Twin overhead camshafts per bank of cylinders
Valves:	Two per cylinder	Three per cylinder
Lubrication:	Dry sump	Dry sump
Compression ratio:	9.7:1	11:1
Power output:	320 bhp at 7600 rpm	450 bhp at 8000 rpm
Chassis		
Gearbox:	Ferrari 5-speed in unit with rear axle	Ferrari 5-speed in unit with rear axle
Front suspension:	Double wishbones and combined coil spring and damper units	Double wishbones and combined coil spring and damper units
Rear suspension:	Lower wishbone, top transverse strut, double radius rods and combined coil spring/damper units	Lower wishbone, top transverse strut, double radius rods and combined coil spring/damper units
Brakes:	Dunlop solid disc	Girling calipers with ventilated discs
Wheels:	15-in. wire-type fitted with 5.50 × 15 tyres at the front and 7.00 × 15 at the rear	15-in. Campagnolo magnesium with 9.5-in. front and 12.5-in. rear rims. 10.15 × 15

Fuel capacity:	38 gallons
Chassis and body:	Multi-tubular space frame with super-structure enclosing mechanical components. Coupé body

Dimensions

Wheelbase:	7ft. 11in.
Front track:	4ft. 5¼in.
Rear track:	4ft. 4¾in.
Overall length:	13ft. 7½in.
Overall height:	4ft. 0½in.
Overall width	5ft. 7½in.
Minimum ground clearance:	4.9in.
Weight:	1874lb.

tyres at the front and 12.15 × 15 at the rear
44 gallons
Multi-tubular space frame and partial stressed skin construction with open or closed fibreglass body

7ft. 11in.
4ft. 10¾in.
4ft. 9¼in.
13ft. 11½in.
3ft. 4in.
6ft. 4in.
5.4in.
1762lb.

Appendix 4

Specification of the Ford G.T. 40

Engine	*Mk I*	*Mk II*	*Mk IV*
Capacity:	4727 cc (289 cu in.)	6997 cc (427 cu in.)	6997 cc (427 cu in.)
Bore:	102 mm (4.00 in.)	108 mm (4.24 in.)	108 mm (4.24 in.)

	Mk I	Mk II	Mk IV
Stroke:	73 mm (2.87 in.)	96 mm (3.78 in.)	96 mm (3.78 in.)
No. of cylinders:	8 in 90-degree vee formation	8 in 90-degree vee formation	8 in 90-degree vee formation
Carburation:	Four twin-choke Weber 48 mm	Single (1966), twin (1967) Holley four-throat	Twin Holley four-throat
Compression ratio:	12.5:1	10.75:1	10.75:1
Lubrication:	Wet sump	Dry sump	Dry sump
Power output:	390 bhp at 7000 rpm	500 bhp at 6400 rpm	500 bhp at 6400 rpm
Maximum torque:	Approx. 325 lb/ft at 5000 rpm	Approx. 470 lb/ft at 5000 rpm	Approx. 470 lb/ft at 5000 rpm
Chassis			
Gearbox:	Originally 4-speed Colotti, but a 5-speed ZF adopted in 1965; in unit with rear axle	4-speed Ford in unit with rear axle	4-speed Ford in unit with rear axle
Front suspension:	Independent by double wishbones	Independent by double wishbones	Independent by double wishbones
Rear suspension:	Double trailing arms with single transverse top link and lower wishbone	Double trailing arms with single transverse top link and lower wishbone	Double trailing arms with single transverse top link and lower wishbone
Steering:	Rack-and-pinion	Rack-and-pinion	Rack-and-pinion
Brakes:	11.5-in. cast iron discs	12-in. ventilated discs	12-in. ventilated discs
Wheel size, front:	6.00 × 15 in.	8.00 × 15 in.	8.00 × 15 in.
Wheel size, rear:	9.00 × 15 in.	9.50 × 15 in. (12.0 × 15 in., 1967)	12.0 × 15 in.
Fuel capacity:	37 U.S. gallons	42 U.S. gallons	42 U.S. gallons
Body/chassis construction:	Monocoque chassis constructed of thin sheet steel; strength-carrying structure consisting of unitised underbody with torque-		Chassis constructed from expanded aluminium honey-

box side sills; front and rear body sections and doors constructed from reinforced fibreglass

comb material sandwiched between aluminium sheets; bonded together with epoxy resin and riveted in areas of highest stress. Front and rear body sections and doors constructed from reinforced fibreglass

Dimensions

Wheelbase:	7ft. 11in.	7ft. 11in.
Front track:	4ft. 6in.	4ft. 9in.
Rear track:	4ft. 6in.	4ft. 8in.
Overall length:	13ft. 9in.	13ft. 7in.
Overall height:	3 ft. 4½in.	3ft. 4½in.
Overall width:	5ft. 10in.	5ft. 10in.
Min. ground clearance	4.8in.	3.94in.
Weight (without fuel)	1835lb	2505lb

		7ft. 11in.
		4ft. 6in.
		4ft. 7in.
		14ft. 3in.
		3ft. 2½in.
		5ft. 10½in.
		4.0in.
		2205lb

Appendix 5

Le Mans Winners on Distance, 1923–1967

First	*Second*	*Third*	*Winner's speed (mph)*
1923			
A. Lagache/R. Leonard (Chenard-Walcker)	R. Bachman/C. Dauvergne (Chenard-Walcker)	de Tornaco/P. Gros (Bignan)	57.21

First	Second	Third	Winner's speed (mph)
1924 J. Duff/F. C. Clement (Bentley)	H. Stoffel/E. Brisson (Lorraine-Dietrich)	H. de Courcelles/A. Rossignol (Lorraine-Dietrich)	53.78
1925 H. de Courcelles/A. Rossignol (Lorraine-Dietrich)	J. Chassagne/S. C. H. Davis (Sunbeam)	H. Stalter/E. Brisson (Lorraine-Dietrich)	57.84
1926 R. Bloch/A. Rossignol (Lorraine-Dietrich)	G. de Courcelles/M. Mongin (Lorraine-Dietrich)	H. Stalter/E. Brisson (Lorraine-Dietrich)	66.08
1927 J. D. Benjafield/S. C. H. Davis (Bentley)	A. de Victor/J. Hasley (Salmson)	L. Desveaux/F. Vallon S.C.A.P.)	61.35
1928 W. Barnato/B. Rubin (Bentley)	R. Bloch/E. Brisson (Stutz)	H. Stoffel/A. Rossignol (Chrysler)	69.11
1929 W. Barnato/Sir H. R. S. Birkin (Bentley)	G. Kidston/J. Dunfee (Bentley)	H. d'Erlanger/J. D. Benjafield (Bentley)	73.63
1930 W. Barnato/G. Kidston (Bentley)	F. C. Clement/R. Watney (Bentley)	B. E. Lewis/H. S. Eaton (Talbot)	75.88

APPENDIX 5

Year	Drivers (Car)	Co-drivers (Car)	Speed
1931	Earl Howe/Sir H. R. S. Birkin (Alfa Romeo)	B. Ivanowski/H. Stoffel (Mercedes-Benz)	T. Rose-Richards/A. Saunders-Davis (Talbot)	78.13
1932	R. Sommer/L. Chinetti (Alfa Romeo)	F. Cortese/G. B. Guidotti (Alfa Romeo)	B. E. Lewis/T. Rose-Richards (Talbot)	76.48
1933	R. Sommer/T. Nuvolari (Alfa Romeo)	L. Chinetti/P. Varent (Alfa Romeo)	B. E. Lewis/T. Rose-Richards (Alfa Romeo)	81.40
1934	L. Chinetti/P. Etancelin (Alfa Romeo)	J. Sébilleau/G. Delaroche (Riley)	F. W. Dixon/C. Paul (Riley)	74.75
1935	J. S. Hindmarsh/L. Fontes (Lagonda)	M. Heldé/H. Stoffel (Alfa Romeo)	G. E. C. Martin/C. Brackenbury (Aston Martin)	77.85
1937	J. P. Wimille/R. Benoist (Bugatti)	J. Paul/M. Mongin (Delahaye)	R. Dreyfus/H. Stoffel (Delahaye)	85.13
1938	E. Chaboud/J. Tremoulet (Delahaye)	G. Serraud/Y. Giraud-Cabantous (Delahaye)	J. Prenant/A. Morel (Lago-Talbot)	82.36
1939	J. P. Wimille/P. Veyron (Bugatti)	L. Gerard/G. Monneret (Delage)	A. Dobson/C. Brackenbury (Lagonda)	86.30

First	Second	Third	Winner's speed (mph)
1949 L. Chinetti/Lord Selsdon (Ferrari)	H. Louveau/J. Jover (Delage)	N. Culpan/H. J. Aldington (Frazer-Nash)	82.27
1950 L. Rosier/J. L. Rosier (Talbot)	P. Meyrat/G. Mairesse (Lago-Talbot)	S. Allard/T. Cole (Allard)	89.73
1951 P. D. Walker/P. N. Whitehead (Jaguar)	P. Meyrat/G. Mairesse (Lago-Talbot)	L. Macklin/E. Thompson (Aston Martin)	93.50
1952 H. Lang/F. Riess (Mercedes-Benz)	T. Helfrich/N. Niedermayer (Mercedes-Benz)	L. G. Johnson/T. H. Wisdom (Nash-Healey)	96.67
1953 A. P. Rolt/J. D. Hamilton (Jaguar)	S. Moss/P. D. Walker (Jaguar)	P. Walters/J. Fitch (Cunningham)	105.85
1954 J. F. Gonzalez/M. Trintignant (Ferrari)	A. P. Rolt/J. D. Hamilton (Jaguar)	W. Spear/S. Johnston (Cunningham)	105.15
1955 J. M. Hawthorn/I. Bueb (Jaguar)	P. Collins/P. Frère (Aston Martin)	J. Claes/J. Swaters (Jaguar)	107.07

1956	S. Moss/P. Collins (Aston Martin)	O. Gendebien/M. Trintignant (Ferrari)	104.46
R. Flockhart/N. Sanderson (Jaguar)			
1957	N. Sanderson/J. Lawrence (Jaguar)	J. Lucas/'Jean Marie' (Jaguar)	113.85
R. Flockhart/I. Bueb (Jaguar)			
1958	A. G. Whitehead/P. Whitehead (Aston Martin)	J. Behra/H. Herrmann (Porsche)	106.20
P. Hill/O. Gendebien (Ferrari)			
1959	M. Trintignant/P. Frère (Aston Martin)	'Beurlys'/'Elde' (Ferrari)	112.57
R. Salvadori/C. Shelby (Aston Martin)			
1960	R. Rodriguez/A. Pilette (Ferrari)	J. Clark/R. Salvadori (Aston Martin)	109.19
P. Frère/O. Gendebien (Ferrari)			
1961	M. Parkes/W. Mairesse (Ferrari)	P. Noblet/P. Guichet (Ferrari)	115.90
P. Hill/O. Gendebien (Ferrari)			
1962	P. Noblet/J. Guichet (Ferrari)	'Elde'/'Beurlys' (Ferrari)	115.24
P. Hill/O. Gendebien (Ferrari)			
1963	'Beurlys'/G. Langlois van Ophem (Ferrari)	M. Parkes/A. Maglioli (Ferrari)	118.10
L. Scarfiotti/L. Bandini (Ferrari)			

First	Second	Third	Winner's speed (mph)
1964 J. Guichet/N. Vaccarella (Ferrari)	G. Hill/J. Bonnier (Ferrari)	J. Surtees/L. Bandini (Ferrari)	121.55
1965 M. Gregory/J. Rindt (Ferrari	P. Dumay/G. Gosselin (Ferrari)	W. Mairesse/'Beurlys' (Ferrari)	121.09
1966 B. McLaren/C. Amon (Ford)	K. Miles/D. Hulme (Ford)	R. Bucknum/R. Hutcherson (Ford)	126.01
1967 A. J. Foyt/D. Gurney (Ford)	M. Parkes/L. Scarfiotti (Ferrari)	W. Mairesse/'Beurlys' (Ferrari)	132.49

Index

Abarth-Simca car, 88
A.C. Cars, 47–56, 60
AC Ace car, 30, 47, 48, 52
Adamich, Andreas de, 98, 99, 140, 145
Adler car, 19
Aldington brothers, 121
Alfa Corse, 28
Alfa Romeo, 11, 18, 19, 21, 24–28, 29, 32, 95
  P1 Grand Prix car, 25
  P2 Grand Prix car, 17, 26
  8C-2300, 17, 18, 26–27
  Monoposto, 27–28
  Bi-motore, 25
  8C-2900B, 18
  158, 31, 32
  3·5-litre coupé, 32
  Guilia, 40
  Tipo 33, 40, 140, 144, 145, 146, 148
Alfieri, Guilo, 105
Allard cars, 20, 21, 46
Allard, Sydney, 20
Alpine cars, 154
Alvis Company, 74
Amon, Chris, 97, 100, 101, 103, 106, 107, 127, 131, 137, 139, 142, 148, 149, 152
Andretti, Mario, 116, 118, 127, 130, 138, 140, 147, 149, 150
Arcangeli, Luigi, 27
Argentine Grand Prix, 1958, 36
Ariès car, 14, 16
ASA car, 130
Ascari, Alberto, 29, 32, 34
Aston Martin, 11, 21, 35, 36, 60, 65, 79, 81, 136, 137
  DB2 car, 19, 20, 22, 60
  DB3S, 22, 46–47, 69
  DBR1, 22, 47
  DBR4/250, 47
  DB6, 136
  V-8 engine, 136–137, 151
ATS cars, 40, 41, 84, 106
Attwood, Richard, 54, 65, 78, 80, 83, 85, 100, 128, 138, 140, 142, 143, 145, 148
Austin-Healey cars, 99, 100
Auto Avio Costruzioni, 29
Auto Union cars, 19, 28, 36

Baghetti, Giancarlo, 78, 81, 98, 99, 107, 121, 123, 148
Bandini, Lorenzo, 74, 76, 78, 83, 86, 97, 98, 99, 102, 108, 120, 121, 122, 123, 128, 137, 141, 142, 144
Baracca, Francesco, 24
Barnato, Wolf, 16, 17
Bazzi, Luigi, 25
Behra, Jean, 39
Belgian Grand Prix, 128 (1966), 152 (1967)
Belgian 24 hours Touring Car Grand Prix, 17 (1928), 17 (1929), 31 (1949)
Beltoise, Jean-Pierre, 85
Benjafield, Dr J. D., 14
Benoist, Robert, 18
Bentley cars, 13, 14, 16, 17, 18
Bentley, W. O., 13, 22, 137
Berthon, Darrell, 14
'Beurlys', 56, 76, 83, 88, 103, 108, 128, 137, 142, 148, 149, 153
Bianchi, Lucien, 76, 102, 103, 127, 130, 138, 139, 142, 143, 147, 149
Bignan car, 14
Biondetti, Clemente, 18
Birkin, Sir Henry, 17
Biscaldi, Giampero, 98, 102, 108
Bizzarini, Giotto, 105
Bizzarini car, 141
Bloch, Robert, 16
BOAC '500', Brands Hatch, 1967, 152–153
Boller, A., 103
Bolton, Peter, 52, 54
Bondurant, Bob, 55, 81, 99, 104, 107, 116, 118, 120, 128
Bonnier, Joakim, 78, 80, 86, 87, 97, 102, 106, 107, 115, 124, 125, 126
Borzacchini, Baconin, 27
Bouriat, Guy, 16
Bowmaker-Yeoman racing team, 63
Brabham, Jack, 37, 66, 152
Brands Hatch meeting, August, 1963, 65
Brescia Grand Prix, 140, 29
Brisson, Edouard, 16
Bristol engines, 48; cars, 95
BRM, 37, 41, 72, 78, 129, 137

INDEX

Broadley, Eric, 62, 63, 65, 66, 67, 68, 69, 75, 89, 104, 110, 135, 136
Broadley, Graham, 62
Brock, Pete, 53
Brown, David, 19
Bucknum, Ronnie, 104–105, 117, 127, 131, 138, 147, 148, 149, 150, 152
Buell, Temple, 47
Buenos Aires 1000 kms race, 1954, 46
Bugatti cars, 18, 19; Type 51, 27; Type 251, 29–30
Bugatti, Ettore, 27

Cadillac cars, 20
Camoradi Racing Team, 105
Campari, Giuseppe, 27
Canadian Sports Car Grand Prix, 1965, 117
Caracciola, Rudolph, 17
Casner, Lloyd, 17
Casona, 98
Castellotti, Eugenio, 33, 34, 45
CD cars, 130
Centro-Sud, Scuderia, 37, 47, 74
Chaparral cars, 93, 94, 95, 113–115, 116, 117, 121, 124–126, 130, 133, 137, 138, 139, 140–141, 142, 143, 144–153
Chapman, Colin, 37, 75
Chassagne, Jean, 14
Chenard-Walcker car, 14, 19
Chevrolet Corvette car, 47, 84, 114; engines, 93, 114, 133, 136, 137, 141
Chinetti, Luigi, 19, 31, 44, 84, 109
Chitti, Carlo, 37, 40
Chrysler cars, 16; engines, 20, 48
Claes, Johnny, 103
Clark, Jim, 39, 87, 138
Clement, Frank, 13
CMN cars, 23
Cobra cars, 46–56, 76, 79, 81, 84, 87, 89, 92, 104, 112, 116
Cole, Ed, 47
Colombo, Giaocchino, 28, 29, 30, 31
Colotti, Valerio, 68
Cooper, John, 36
Cooper cars, 30, 36–38, 47, 66, 106; Monaco, 38, 96; Maserati, 128; Oldsmobile, 87
Coppa Acerbo race, 1924, 24
Cortese, Franco, 30
Coundley, John, 88
Courage, Piers, 130, 148
Coventry-Climax engines, 36, 37, 41, 63
Cunningham, Briggs, 20
Cunningham cars, 20, 21, 56, 79, 95
Cussons, Nick, 120

Daily Express Trophy meeting, Silverstone, 1963, 64–65
Davis, Cliff, 48

Davis, Colin, 100, 122
Davis, S. C. H., 14
Daytona Continental Grand Touring race, 1963, 51; 2000 kms race, 52 (1964), 55, 92 (1965); 24 hours race, 115–116 (1966), 137–140 (1967)
Delage cars, 18, 19
Delahaye cars, 18, 19
Deserti, 98
Detroit Automobile Co, 58
Donohue, Mark, 116, 117, 127, 129, 139, 147, 148
Dragoni, Eugenio, 116, 117, 127, 129, 139, 147, 148
Duesenberg cars, 18
Duff, John, 13
Dumay, Pierre, 76, 79, 103, 108–109, 128
du Pont cars, 16
Durand, Georges, 13
Duray, Leon, 59

Eagle cars, 112
Ecurie Ecosse, 21, 35, 52
Edgar, John, 47
'Elde', 103
English, F., Ltd, 120, 127
Epstein, J., 143
Essex Wire Corporation, 111, 116, 120, 121, 124, 127, 135
European Grand Prix, 1924, 26

Fangio, Juan, 32
Fantuzzi, 52
Faroux, Charles, 13
Ferrari, Alfredo, 23
Ferrari, Dino, 38
Ferrari, Enzo, 11, 23–35, 36–45, 72, 73, 74, 91, 92, 96, 97, 115, 128, 144, 145
Ferrari, Scuderia, 11, 17, 24, 25, 26–35
Ferrari cars, 11, 20, 21, 22, 30–45, 48, 52, 53, 57, 72–88, 91–110, 115–131, 132–133, 137–153, 154, 155
Grand Prix cars:
4·5-litre V-12, 31
Dino V-6, 37, 38
1·5-litre V-6, 38, 40
Sports Cars:
Tipo 815, 29
1·5-litre V-12, 30
2-litre V-12, 19, 30–31, 48
4·1-litre V-12, 20, 31–32
4·5-litre V-12, 31–32
4·9-litre V-12, 21, 32, 33, 104
3-litre V-12, 32
2-litre 4-cyl, 33
3-litre 4-cyl, 33
4·4-litre 6-cyl, 33, 47
3-litre V-12 'Testa Rossa', 35, 41, 52
Prototypes:
246/SP V-6, 39, 41

INDEX

248/SP V-8, 40–41
4-litre V-12, 41
250/P V-12, 41, 42, 72
330/P V-12, 41, 55, 73–74, 78, 79
250/275LM V-12, 55, 56, 72–73, 79, 83, 91, 111
275/P V-12, 73–74, 76, 78, 79
275/P2 V-12, 91–92
330/P2, 91–92
365/P V-12, 91
330/P3 V-12, 116, 120
330/P4 V-12, 132
330/P3/4, 132
Dino V-6, 40, 96–97, 102, 107, 117, 120
Grand Touring:
  250GT, 35, 52, 72
  330GT, 42
  250GTO, 42, 52, 53, 54, 55, 72, 76, 77, 83, 86, 91, 130
  250/275 LM, *See* Prototypes above
  275GTB, 55, 56, 91, 92, 102, 151
Fiat, 25, 26, 34, 44, 57, 115
Filipinetti, Scuderia, 44, 56, 87, 91, 97, 103, 104, 107, 120, 121, 123, 127, 128, 142, 144, 145, 150, 151
Fitch, John, 46
Fontes, Luis, 18
Ford, Henry, 58–59
Ford II, Henry, 131
Ford, 11–12, 44, 45, 46–56, 57–71, 72–88, 89–91, 115, 121, 123–124, 126–131, 137–153
  26 hp, 59
  'Arrow', 59
  '999', 59
  Model T, 59
  Cougar II, 49
  Mustang I, 60–61, 70
  105 E Anglia, 60
  Taunus 12M, 60
  Cortina, 116
  GT 40, 56, 59–71, 89–91, 92–110, 111–112
  GT 40 Mk II, 90–91, 112–113, 114, 134
  J-Car, 113–114, 133
  GT 40 Mk III, 133–134
  GT 40 Mk IV, 133–134
  V-8 30 hp engine, 53
  Zephyr engine, 48
  Galaxie engine, 53
Ford Advanced Vehicles Ltd, 66, 89, 100, 104, 107, 109, 134
Ford-France, 100–101, 102, 104, 120, 121, 123, 127, 150, 151, 153
Forghieri, Mauro, 125
Fornaca, 25
Foyt, A. J., 117, 139, 140, 141, 147, 148, 150
Francorchamps, Ecurie, 97, 100, 102, 103, 123, 128, 137

Frazer Nash cars, 121
French Grand Prix, 29 (1956), 123 (1961)
Frère, Paul, 47
Frua, 50

Gardner, Frank, 117, 118, 123, 127, 129, 138, 147, 148
Gendebien, Olivier, 39
General Motors, 114, 115
Ginther, Richie, 38, 41, 78, 80, 83, 84, 85, 93, 128, 129, 130, 138
Gobron-Brillié car, 59
Gonzalez, Froilan, 20, 33
Gordini cars, 21
Gosselin, G., 103, 108
Grant, Jerry, 53–54, 92, 116, 119, 127, 128, 137
Gregory, Ken, 114
Gregory, Masten, 78, 80, 83, 108, 109, 121, 128, 137
Guichet, Jean, 78, 97, 98, 101, 102, 107, 108, 110, 121, 123, 128, 137, 139, 148
Gurney, Dan, 53, 54, 55, 81, 92, 93, 112, 116, 117, 119, 127, 129, 130, 138, 139, 147, 148, 149, 150

Hall, Jim, 93, 94, 95, 114, 124, 126, 133, 138, 140, 143, 146, 147, 150
Hamilton, Duncan, 33
Hansgen, Walter, 116, 117, 120, 140
Hanstein, Hushke von, 124
Hawkins, Paul, 127, 129, 143, 144, 147–148, 150, 152, 153
Healey (Nash-powered), 20, 21; (Coventry-Climax-powered), 155
Herrmann, Hans, 139
Hill, Claude, 60
Hill, Graham, 55, 76, 77, 80, 81, 83, 85, 86, 87, 88, 91, 94, 101, 105, 117, 118, 127, 128, 130
Hill, Phil, 41, 51, 53, 54, 76, 78, 80, 81, 83, 93, 100, 101, 103, 106, 107, 115, 124, 125, 126, 127, 137, 138, 144, 146, 147, 148, 149, 152
Hindmarsh, John, 18
Hissom, 94
Hoare, Colonel Ronnie, 76, 77, 101, 120
Hobbs, David, 65, 147, 152
Holbert, Bob, 65, 147, 152
Holman, John, 115, 143
Holman & Moody Inc, 115, 117, 118, 135, 147
Holquist, Bob, 127
Honda cars, 105, 136
Honda S800, 146
Howe, Earl, 17
Hudson, Skip, 78, 81, 84
Hugus, Ed, 52
Hulme, Denis, 127, 129, 131, 147, 149

INDEX

Hutcherson, Dick, 127
Hutton, Barbara, 49

Ickx, Jackie, 138, 143, 145, 147
Ireland, Innes, 55, 76, 77, 79, 82, 97, 104
Irwin, Chris, 147
Iso Grifo car, 76, 84, 95, 105–106
Isotta-Fraschini 'Monterosa' car, 31
Italian Grand Prix, 26 (1931), 39 (1961)
Ivanowski, Boris, 17

Jaguar cars, 11, 32, 33, 35, 57, 78; XK120, 46; C-type, 46; D-type, 21, 33; E-type, 72, 76, 81, 84
Jano, Vittorio, 17, 25–26, 27, 28, 32, 34, 38
Jennings, Bruce, 94, 138, 146
Johnson, Bob, 53, 55, 138, 146
Jowett cars, 60
JW Automotive Ltd, 134, 135, 140

Keck, 55
Kidston, Glen, 17
King Cobra car, 96
Klass, Günther, 145, 148, 150
Klerk, Peter de, 121, 147
Kolb, Charles, 139

Lagonda cars, 18, 21; 4½-litre V-12, 137
Laly, 14
Lamborghini, Ferraccio, 40
Lamborghini cars, 40, 42, 105
Lampredi, Aurelio, 31, 32, 34
Lancia cars, 21, 28, 34, 44, 95; Aprilia, 60; Aurelia, 33; V-6 sports, 32, 33; D.50 Grand Prix car, 34–35; Flavia, 76
Lancia, Scuderia, 32
Le Mans race, 13–14 (1923), 14 (1924), 14 (1925), 14 (1926), 14–16 (1927), 16 (1928), 16 (1929), 17 (1930), 17, 18 (1931), 17, 18 (1932), 17, 18 (1933), 17, 18 (1934), 18 (1935), 18 (1937), 18 (1938), 18 (1939), 18–19 (1949), 19, 20 (1950), 19–20, 21 (1951), 20 (1952), 21 (1953), 21 (1954), 21, 22 (1955), 21, 22 (1956), 21 (1957), 21, 22 (1958), 21 (1959), 22 (1961), 52, 65 (1963), 54, 77–82 (1964), 56, 102–109 (1965), 126–131 (1966), 146–151 (1967)
Le Mans Test Weekend, 74–75 (1964); 95–96 (1965); 115, 119–120 (1966); 141–142 (1967)
Levegh, Pierre, 20, 21
Ligier, Guy, 100, 104, 121, 147
Lindner, Peter, 88
Lister, Brian, 82
Lister-Jaguar car, 76, 78
Lola cars, 62–65, 140; GT, 63–65, 113; T.70 Group 7, 89, 110; Aston Martin, 135–137, 145, 146, 149, 151; Chevrolet, 143, 151, 152
Lorraine-Dietrich cars, 14
Lotus cars, 37, 38, 63, 72, 92, 103, 114, 137
19, 38
Elite, 65
30, 87, 93
40, 110
Lunn, Roy, 60, 61, 66, 67, 68, 69, 75, 90, 106, 113, 133
Lyons, Sir William, 33

Macklin, Lance, 20
Maggs, Tony, 65, 82
Maglioli, Umberto, 75, 76, 78, 81, 84, 97, 104
Mairesse, Willy, 41, 56, 88, 97, 100, 108, 121, 123, 137, 142, 143
Mann, Alan, 56, 115–117, 118, 119, 120, 123, 127, 129
Maranello Concessionaires Ltd, 44, 54, 76, 78, 80, 83, 84, 87, 88, 97, 100, 101, 106, 108, 110, 120, 123, 124, 132, 142, 150
Maserati cars, 27, 28, 35, 41, 42, 47; 250F Grand Prix car, 29, 47; Mistrale, 50; 'Bird-cage', 61; 5-litre V-8, 79, 84, 86; Tipo 65, 105
Massimino, Alberto, 29, 34
Mathis cars, 26
Matra cars, 128; BRM, 129, 130, 141; Ford, 141
McClusky, Roger, 150
McDonald, Dave, 51, 53
McLaren, Bruce, 40, 66, 76, 78, 81, 83, 84, 85, 93, 95, 97, 101, 106, 107, 131, 136, 138, 139, 140, 148, 149, 150
McLaren cars; Oldsmobile, 110; Formula One, 110
Mecom, John, 92, 94
Mercedes-Benz, 19, 28, 33, 34, 48, 95; SSKL, 17; 300S, 20; 300SL, 20; 300SLR, 21
Meregali, 24
Merosi, Giuseppe, 24, 25, 26
Miles, Ken, 51, 89, 92, 93, 95, 97, 104, 107, 112, 116, 118, 129, 131, 134
Mille Miglia, 17 (1928); 17 (1929); 27 (1931); 31 (1950); 31, 32 (1951); 31 (1952); 31, 32 (1953); 32, 33 104 (1954); 35 (1956)
Minozzi, Giovanni, 29
Mirage car, 135, 141, 142, 143, 144, 145
Mitter, Gerhard, 100, 122, 123, 141, 142, 146, 147, 149, 152, 153, 155
Monaco Grand Prix, 34 (1955); 36 (1958); 38 (1960); 144 (1967)
Monza 1000 km race, 55, 96–98 (1965); 120–121, 128 (1966); 141–142 (1967)

INDEX

Mortemart, 106
Moss, Stirling, 52, 84
Mugello, Circuit of, 1921, 24
Muir, Brian, 127, 130
Müller, Hans, 97, 121, 123, 144
Musso, Luigi, 97, 121, 123, 144

Nash-Healey car, 20, 21
National Belge, Équipe, 44, 76, 87–88, 132, 142, 153
Nazzaro, Felice, 24
Neerpasch, J., 55
North American Racing Team, 19, 31, 41, 44, 73, 78, 83, 88, 92, 108, 109, 110, 116–118, 124, 130, 132, 137, 139, 142, 150
Nurbürgring 1000 km race, 32 (1953); 39 (1961); 41 (1962); 42, 65 (1963); 54, 75–77, 79 (1964); 100–102 (1965); 124–126, 129 (1966); 145–146 (1967)
Nuvolari, Tazio, 27, 28

Oldfield, Barney, 59
Olthoff, Bob, 55, 65
Ophem, Langlois van, 79, 83

Paget, Hon. Dorothy, 17
Panamericana Mexico race, 1954, 32–33
Paris 1000 km race, 55, 87 (1964); 153 (1967)
Parkes, Michael, 54, 74, 78, 97, 98, 100, 108, 110, 116, 117, 118, 120, 121, 122, 123, 124, 125, 126, 128, 130, 137, 139, 141, 142, 143, 148, 149, 152
Parma-Poggio di Berceto Hill Climb, 1919, 24
Patria, Franco, 88
Patrick, 141
Patterson, Charles H., 57
Pescara Four Hours race, 1961, 39
'Philippe', 16
Pike, Roy, 130
Pinin Farina, 32, 42, 52
Piper, David, 55, 79, 97, 100, 103, 123, 138, 139, 140, 142, 143, 152
Pon, Ben, 55
Porsche cars, 41, 42, 79
 904, 54, 55, 73, 75, 76, 84, 99, 100, 102, 109, 118, 119
 906 Carrera 6, 121, 124
 8-cyl Prototypes, 123, 124, 129, 130, 139, 140, 141, 142, 143, 144, 146, 152
Protheroe, Dick, 88
Pucci, 54

Rangoni, Lotario, 29
Redman, Brian, 124
Rees, Alan, 143

Remington, Phil, 89
Reventlow, Lance, 49
Revson, Peter, 124, 139
Rheims 12 Hours race, 55, 83–87 (1964); 110 (1965); 151–152 (1967)
Ricart, Wilfredo, 28
Rimini, Giorgio, 25
Rindt, Jochen, 76, 79, 84, 108, 109, 125, 128, 142
Rodriguez, Pedro, 53, 78, 80, 81, 84, 88, 93, 94, 110, 116, 117, 129, 137, 138, 139, 140, 142
Rolland, 145
Rolls-Royce, 17, 42
Rolt, A. P. R., 33
Romeo, Nicola, 24, 25
Rose-Richards, Tim, 18
Rosier, Jean-Louis, 19
Rosier, Louis, 19
Rover-BRM car, 105
Rubin, Bernard, 16
Ruby, Lloyd, 92, 116, 141, 149

St Ambroeus, Scuderia, 120, 121
Salmon, Mike, 79, 123
Salvadori, Roy, 21, 47, 63, 96
Sanderson, Ninian, 52
Savio, Circuit of 1923, 24
Scaglietti, 42
Scarab sports car, 49
Scarfiotti, Lodovico, 41, 74, 76, 78, 87, 88, 97, 98, 99, 101, 107, 117, 120, 121, 123, 125, 128, 130, 137, 139, 142, 144, 145, 149, 152
Schlesser, Jo, 54, 55, 71, 78, 80, 82, 85, 88, 137, 139, 150
Scott, Skip, 124
Sears, Jack, 54, 55, 56
Sebring 12 Hours race, 39 (1961); 41, 51 (1963); 53 (1964); 92–95 (1965); 116–119 (1966); 140–141 (1967)
Selsdon, Lord, 19, 31
Serenissima car, 40, 104
Sharp, Hap, 93, 114, 145, 146
Shelby, Carroll, 21, 46–56, 81, 89, 92, 96, 97, 99, 101, 104, 107, 109, 111, 116, 118, 120, 130, 147
Siffert, Joseph, 85, 139, 142, 152
Simon, André, 79
Simone, Colonel, 105
Sivocci, Ugo, 23, 25
Slotemaker, 55
Societa Torinese Automobili Rapid, 25
Sommer, Raymond, 18
Spa, Grand Prix de, 1965, 100; 1000 km race, 123–124, 126 (1966); 142–144 (1967)
Spanish Grand Prix, 1954, 34
Spence, Mike, 137, 138, 140, 142, 143, 145, 146, 147, 149, 152

INDEX

Sports Car Championship, 31, 32 (1953); 33 (1954); 35 (1956); 35 (1957); 35 (1958); 22, 137 (1959); 39 (1961)
Spychiger, Tommy, 91, 97
Stewart, Jackie, 87, 88, 101, 105, 117, 118, 138, 152
Stoffel, Henri 17
Stommelen, 145
Stutz cars, 16, 17
Sunbeam Tiger car, 81–82
Superleggera Touring, 30
Surtees, John, 41, 63, 65, 74, 76, 77, 78, 80, 83, 85, 86, 93, 97, 101, 106, 107, 108, 110, 120, 124, 125, 126, 128, 136, 137, 146, 147, 152
Sutcliffe, Peter, 79, 124, 150, 152
Swallow, William, 54

Talbot (British) cars, 18
Talbot (French) cars, 18, 19, 20, 21
Targa Florio, 24 (1919); 24 (1920); 39 (1961); 41 (1962); 42 (1963); 53, 74 (1964); 98–100 (1965); 121–123 (1966); 144–145 (1967)
Tatra car, 31
Tavoni, 40
Taylor, Sid, 152
Thompson, Dick, 127, 138, 142, 143, 145
Thompson, Eric, 20
Tojeiro, John, 30, 47, 48
Tourist Trophy race, 1964, 55, 87
Trintignant, Maurice, 33, 79

Trips, Wolfgang von, 39

Udy, Mike de, 121, 143
Vaccarella, Nino, 41, 74, 76, 77, 78, 82, 84, 97, 98, 99, 102, 121, 142, 144
Vandervell, G. A., 135
Varzi, Achille, 27
Venturi, 145
Villoresi, Luigi, 32, 34
Vitafoam Racing Team, 99
Volkswagen car, 57
Volpi, Count, 40

Walker, Peter, 20
Walker, Rob, 104, 107
Weber, Edoardo, 28
Weber, Roby, 141
Werner, Christian, 17
Weymann, Charles, 16
Whitehead, Peter, 20
Whitmore, Sir John, 99, 107, 118, 121, 123, 129
Williams, Jonathon, 145, 152
Willment, John, 54, 127, 134, 148
Wimille, Jean-Pierre, 18
Winton car, 58, 59
Wright, Mike, 88
Wyer, John, 65, 66, 76, 89, 95, 96, 99, 104, 111, 123, 134, 135

Yorke, David, 135